CROSSING
WITH THE
CLARKS

A HISTORY OF A SCOTTISH FAMILY'S FERRIES
AND TAVERN ON THE SUSQUEHANNA

VICTOR HART

SUNBURY
PRESS

Mechanicsburg, PA USA

Published by Sunbury Press, Inc.
Mechanicsburg, Pennsylvania

www.sunburypress.com

For information about special discounts for bulk purchases, please contact Sunbury Press Orders Dept. at (855) 338-8359 or orders@sunburypress.com.

To request one of our authors for speaking engagements or book signings, please contact Sunbury Press Publicity Dept. at publicity@sunburypress.com.

ISBN: 978-1-62006-239-5 (Trade paperback)

Library of Congress Control Number: 2019957361

FIRST SUNBURY PRESS EDITION: January 2020

Product of the United States of America
0 1 1 2 3 5 8 13 21 34 55

Set in Adobe Garamond
Designed by Crystal Devine
Cover by Lawrence Knorr
Edited by Lawrence Knorr

Continue the Enlightenment!

*Dedicated to my loving wife, Jessica,
without whose encouragement and patience,
this book would not have been possible.*

CONTENTS

LIST OF FIGURES

ACKNOWLEDGMENTS

Crossing with the Clarks was a three-part study:

- A history of the Clark family, their ferries and tavern
- A preliminary architectural study of Clark's Tavern in Duncannon, Pennsylvania
- An archaeological study of the tavern grounds.

The research for the history in this book would not have been possible without the help of the staff at the following institutions: Cumberland County Historical Society and Archives, Perry Historians, Historical Society of Perry County, Historical Society of Dauphin County, Pennsylvania State Archives and State Library. In addition, the following individuals shared information they researched with the author: Jason Wilson, Max, and Nathan Smith, Barbara Bartos, Janet Taylor, Dennis Hocker, and Jeff and Joan Popchock.

The architectural study in the book would not have been possible without the help of the following: Max and Nathan Smith, David Scott Simpson, Jennifer and Jason Wilson, Roland Finkenbinder, Steven O. Smith, Glenn Vernon, Duane Hammaker, and the Duncannon Borough Council.

The results of the archaeological excavations will not be described in this book, but in a separate report, *Digging for the Clarks*. The report would not have been possible without the following: Tom Prescott, Sis and Roy Clugston, Janet Taylor, Roland Finkenbinder, Krista Haas, Michelle Smith, Max and Nathan Smith, Duane Hammaker, and the Duncannon Borough Council.

A special thanks to my friend, Jason Wilson, for reviewing the manuscript and making suggestions on how to improve it.

PART I

A HISTORY OF CLARK'S FERRIES AND TAVERN

INTRODUCTION

In 1814, as young Benjamin Long came ashore from one of Clark's Ferries, he looked back across the Susquehanna River into a terrific storm. The ferry had carried him, his mother, his siblings, a wagon, and the family's money chest across the Susquehanna River from Dauphin County to what was then Cumberland County. After putting ashore at Clark's Tavern Landing, Benjamin looked back across the river for his father, David Long. David was supposed to have followed on a second Clark's Ferry when a fierce storm arose on the Susquehanna. The storm limited Benjamin's visibility to less than halfway across. When he, his mother, and siblings could not see the ferry carrying his father, they "feared that the father and the second wagon were caught in the storm on the river and probably drowned." As a result, the family spent a night in their wagon in despair. It was not until the next morning, after the storm had subsided, that the family's fears were put to rest. When Benjamin came out of the wagon, he saw his mother waving to his father, standing on the opposite bank of the river. Fortunately, the ferry carrying David and their other wagon had not left the Dauphin County side of the river before the storm hit. After Benjamin and his family left, one of the ferrymen on his father's ferry "suggested that they first visit a settler's house nearby for a dram," i.e., a drink of whiskey. By the time David and his ferry crew returned to their ferry, the fierce storm and darkness had set in. As a result, David's ferry crew decided to wait until the next morning to cross the river. The next day, David and his family were reunited when he crossed the river unimpeded.[1]

Benjamin and his family had crossed on Clark's Ferries just below the confluence of the Susquehanna and Juniata Rivers (See Figure 1). Native Americans had been crossing at the junction for over a millennium. Early European ferrymen such as James Baskin, Marcus Huling, and Francis Ellis had established ferry lines across the confluence from as early as 1767.[2] In the late 1700s, when the Clark family arrived, they must have seen the junction of the Susquehanna and Juniata Rivers as an opportunity to establish thriving ferry and tavern businesses. After the Northwest Territory opened in 1787, a wave of pioneer expansion took place. New turnpikes were constructed to accommodate the ever-increasing number

FIGURE 1: CONFLUENCE OF THE SUSQUEHANNA AND JUNIATA RIVERS
(Courtesy of the Tri-County Regional Planning Commision)

of settlers moving west. The history of Clark's successful ferry and tavern businesses reflect an increase in demand for ferry and tavern services brought about by increased western migration and new road systems at the turn of the nineteenth century.

HISTORIC PERIODS

The previous account of the Long family crossing the Susquehanna River on two of Clark's Ferries took place in 1814. This occurred during Clark's peak ferry and tavern period. By 1814, the Clark family had been running a ferry across the Susquehanna for twenty-seven years. The history of Clark's Ferries and their associated tavern can be broken down into the following periods:

- Pre-ferry and tavern, 1766–1787
- Early ferry and tavern, 1787–1802
- Peak ferry and tavern, 1802–1836
- Post-ferry, 1836–1875
- Post-tavern, 1875–present

1

PRE-FERRY AND TAVERN PERIOD
(1766–1787)

In 1766, pioneer Samuel Goudy established his homestead on property that would later become the location for John Clark's Cumberland County tavern and ferry landing. Two years later, in 1768, Samuel surveyed the two hundred and fifteen acres and thirty-eight perches of his homestead (See Figure 2). It was not until 1774, however, that John and Thomas Penn warranted him the land. In the warrant, Samuel called the property "Silver Spring."[1]

When he settled at Silver Spring, Samuel Goudy would have been a frontier farmer. His survival would have depended mostly on hunting, fishing, and gathering wild plants. By 1785, when he put Silver Spring up for sale, he had become at least a yeoman farmer, growing all or almost all of the food he and his family needed to survive.[2]

Evidence of Samuel Goudy having reached the level of subsistence farming can be found in his 1786 Rye Township, Cumberland County tax assessment. In the assessment, he was taxed for two horses and four cows.[3] Further evidence of his having developed to the level of subsistence farming can be found in Samuel's 1785, "Valuable Plantation to Be Sold" advertisement (See Figure 3).[4]

In 1785, for unknown reasons, Samuel and his wife, Sarah, decided to sell Silver Spring. In Carlisle's *Gazette* newspaper, Samuel advertised a "Valuable Plantation to be Sold." Although his original warrant was two hundred and fifteen acres and thirty-eight perches, in his advertisement,

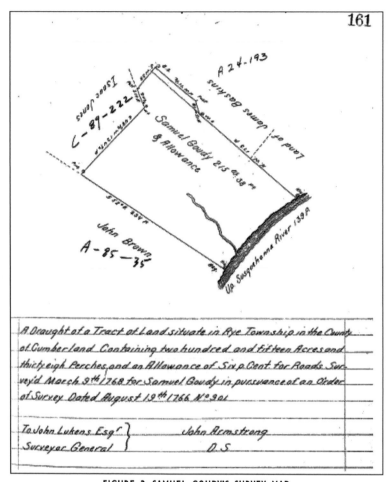

FIGURE 2: SAMUEL GOUDY'S SURVEY MAP
Application Date: August 19, 1766 — Surveyed March 9, 1768 — Warrant to Accept: December 5, 1774

he stated that the property contained two hundred and sixty-nine acres. The number of acres listed for sale by Samuel Goudy was probably a mistake made by the *Gazette*. In Cumberland County's 1786 tax assessment, Goudy is assessed for two hundred and fifteen acres and thirty-eight perches.

In his advertisement, besides listing the number of acres to be sold, Samuel described the property. He stated that there were around 40 acres of "upland cleared." This included "a small piece of meadow cleared, a

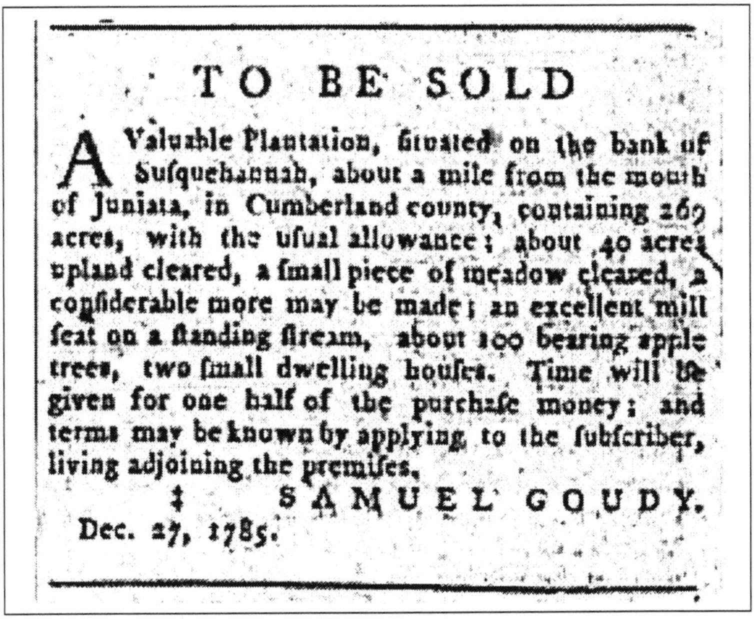

TO BE SOLD

A Valuable Plantation, ſituated on the bank of Suſquehannah, about a mile from the mouth of Juniata, in Cumberland county, containing 269 acres, with the uſual allowance; about 40 acres upland cleared, a ſmall piece of meadow cleared, a conſiderable more may be made; an excellent mill ſeat on a ſtanding ſtream, about 100 bearing apple trees, two ſmall dwelling houſes. Time will be given for one half of the purchaſe money; and terms may be known by applying to the ſubſcriber, living adjoining the premiſes.

SAMUEL GOUDY.
Dec. 27, 1785.

FIGURE 3: VALUABLE PLANTATION TO BE SOLD
The Carlisle Gazette, Number 21, Volume I — Wednesday, December 28, 1785

considerable more may be made." He also described how, on the property, there was a stream that would be an excellent site for a mill. The stream is located on the Clark Street side of the tavern building under 3B Ice Cream's parking lot and is called Clark's Run. Also, he stated that the property contained "100 bearing apple trees."[5] Today, the alley behind the tavern is called Apple Tree Alley, likely named after the apple orchard that was once in the vicinity.

2

EARLY FERRY AND TAVERN PERIOD
(1787–1802)

The Early ferry and tavern period revolves primarily around two men, John Clark and his eldest son, Daniel.[1] John was the financier who bought the property and started Clark's Ferry and tavern businesses, while his son, Daniel, ran them until 1799 when his younger brother, Robert, took charge.

On January 23, 1787, about thirteen months after Goudy's' advertisement in the *Gazette,* John Clark purchased Goudy's property.[2] The property would become the location for John Clark's successful farm, tavern and ferry businesses. It would remain in possession of the Clark family for eighty-two years, until 1869.[3]

After purchasing Silver Spring from Samuel and Sarah Goudy in 1787, it appears that John Clark did not immediately homestead his property. When the property was assessed for taxes by Cumberland County in August of 1787, he was taxed for just the property, but nothing else.[4]

By August of the following year, 1788, tax assessments show John had settled on the property. In addition to the land, he was taxed for two horses and four cows. It is likely his oldest son Daniel, who had arrived from Scotland by 1786, was instrumental in helping his father establish both a farm and ferry.[5]

ALBA GU BRATH (SCOTTISH AND PROUD)

Scotland was the Clark family's homeland. Cumberland County Records state that Daniel Clark had come from Scotland by 1786.[6] Robert Clark, along with his sister, Christina, is listed in the 1850 U.S. Census as having been born in Scotland.[7] In addition, "Native of Scotland" was engraved on Robert Clark's tombstone. Their Scottish connection is further reinforced by the Clark family's religious affiliation with the Presbyterian Church of Scotland. The marriages performed at Clark's Tavern in the 1800s were all performed by Presbyterian ministers.

The motivation for the Clark family coming to America from Scotland is not known. They were perhaps pulled to the United States by a belief that new economic opportunities awaited them. Fortunately, their intuition proved to be correct.

The same year John Clark bought Silver Spring, 1787, the Confederation Congress of the United States passed the Northwest Ordinance. This created the Northwest Territory, which later evolved into the states of Ohio, Michigan, Indiana, Illinois, Wisconsin, and Minnesota.[8] This Ordinance opened new territories beyond Pittsburgh for waves of pioneers. These pioneers needed a means by which they and their belongings could cross the Susquehanna River and a place where they could recuperate from their traveling ordeals. Clark's Ferry and Tavern would help to fill these needs.

At the same time, the Clarks were likely pulled to the United States by economic opportunity; the Highland Clearances in Scotland likely helped to push them out.

The Highland Clearances started in Scotland in the last half of the 18th century. During that period, large landowners in Scotland decided that sheep were more valuable than crofters (tenant farmers) whose families had farmed their lands for hundreds of years. As a result, there was an organized removal of non-landed people.[9] There are two pieces of evidence indicating that the Clark family came from the Scottish Highlands.

First, a gristmill was contracted to be built for Robert Clark and two business partners, William Ramsey and John Boden, in 1810. Ramsey was Deputy Surveyor for Cumberland County and had previously married Robert's sister, Nancy, also known as Ann.[10] Boden was High Sherriff of Cumberland County, who in 1811 married another one of Robert's sisters, Jane.[11] Together, the three partners contracted with John Chisholm to build and run a gristmill for them. Chisholm was from the Scottish Highland city of Inverness. [12]

The second piece of evidence that the Clarks were from the Highlands of Scotland is that in Scotland, Clark families/septs primarily belong to either the Cameron or MacPherson Clans. Both clans and their associated families live along the shores of Loch Ness or Loch Lochy in the Highlands.[13]

EVERY THING HATH A BEGINNING

H.H. Hain, in his *History of Perry County, Pennsylvania*, states, "That the ferry was established in 1788 and that Daniel Clark was the pioneer ferryman." The 1788 date given by Hain is based on a series of notices placed in Harrisburg's newspaper, the *Oracle of Dauphin*. In the notices, ferrymen Francis Ellis, Daniel Clark, and Mathias Flam argued over who had landing rights at Mathias Flam's Landing in Dauphin County.

Ferryman Francis Ellis first posted his argument in a notice in the *Oracle of Dauphin* on June 20, 1800. His notice announced that he had "acquired the privilege of Mathias Flam's [ferry] Landing on the Dauphin shore, opposite his present place of residence, at the mouth of the Juniata . . ." Ellis then went on to say, "Footman, Horsemen, and Wagons will be received at Mr. Flam's and conveyed to this shore with great dispatch and safety."[14] Francis Ellis had established his ferry landing on Duncan's Island across from Flams' during the American Revolutionary War. [15]

In response to Francis Ellis' notice, Daniel Clark wrote a notice of his own in the *Oracle*. On July 1, 1800, Daniel's notice complained that another ferryman named Francis Ellis, ". . . takes the liberty of inviting travelers to Mathias Flam's landing, where he has no right or

privilege . . ." Daniel goes on to say in his notice, ". . . I am still in possession of both sides as formerly, with the same hands, same flats, and same
buildings, ready to receive passengers on both sides." He continued that
he "has conducted this Ferry for twelve years past without the assistance
of Newspaper bombast."[16] Twelve years from the date of the newspaper
printing makes the starting year for Clark's Ferry, 1788.

On July 12, 1800, Mathias Flam, gave a response to Daniel's notice.
Flam's notice in the *Oracle* stated, that ". . . Daniel has forgot the obli-
gations he has been under to the subscriber's lenity . . . as he has been
suffered to conduct the Ferry for these twelve years past . . ."[17] The math
again places 1788 as the starting year for Clarks Ferry. Another document that helps establish 1788 as the starting date for Clark's Ferry was
a 1788 road petition.

A road petition is a formally drawn request to construct a public road
from one location to another. On August 8, 1788, a road petition was filed
in Cumberland County for a road to be built ". . . from George Hamilton's now Hackets, . . . to the plantation formerly occupied & owned by
Capt. Samuel Goudy adjoining the river Susquehannah where a convenient ferry may be had . . ."[18] John Clark had purchased Goudy's "plantation . . . where a convenient ferry may be had" in 1787, the previous year.

The previously mentioned newspaper notices placed by Francis Ellis,
Daniel Clark, and Mathias Flam seem to have been based on some mis-
understanding. At that time, there was not one ferry landing on Flam's
property but two. The two landings were on opposite ends of a fifty-acre
tract originally warranted to Marcus Huling as "Huling's Landing" on
January 12, 1769. Marcus Huling was the first ferryman to run a ferry
across the Susquehanna River from his ferry landing on the east side of
the Susquehanna to what is today Duncan's Island on the west side (See
Figure 4).[19] On the map, Duncan's is named Baskins'.

In 1785, Marcus Huling sold his fifty acres and ferry landing to his
youngest son, Thomas.[20] Although records for the transaction are missing, by 1788, Thomas had turned over the ownership of the fifty acres
and ferry landing to Mathias Flam. Huling's Landing then became Flam's
Landing. It was used as the eastern terminus for Francis Ellis' Ferry, who

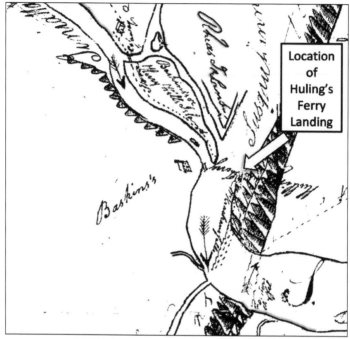

FIGURE 4: MARCUS HULING'S FERRY CROSSING
Part of Wright's to Juniata Map — May 11, 1820

had his landing on Duncan's Island. This was Flam's first and northern ferry landing.

By the time Clark's Ferry was established in 1788, Mathias Flam had established a second ferry landing. It was just above Foster Falls and across from Clark's Tavern on the southern end of his fifty acres. The landing was likely built for the newly established Clark's Ferry.

ROADS AND FERRIES WEST

The same year John and Daniel Clark started their ferry, 1788, the United States Constitution was ratified, and a new United States Government was established. The year before, July 13, 1787, the Confederation Congress passed the Northwest Ordinance creating the Northwest Territory. As a result, pioneers began moving west in larger numbers from the

Atlantic coast. Increasing numbers of settlers left Philadelphia heading for Pittsburgh and the Northwest Territory. Upon leaving Philadelphia, they encountered two problems. The first was traveling on deplorable dirt roads, and the second was crossing the Susquehanna River.

Before the American Revolution, there were only dirt roads between communities in Pennsylvania. Roads between towns and cities were widened dirt paths, usually in bad condition. They had initially been trails made by Indians and later by Europeans on foot or horseback. After the Revolution, with increased numbers of people moving west, the condition of the dirt roads became worse. This was particularly true of the well-traveled road between Philadelphia and Lancaster.[21]

By 1792, traffic on the road had become so heavy, and the road was in such poor condition that enterprising businessmen saw an opportunity to make a profit from improving it. They formed the Philadelphia and Lancaster Turnpike Company. When finished in 1794, the turnpike was the first crushed-stone-paved road in the newly formed United States. The ease of traveling on the improved road encouraged more pioneers to head west.[22]

After arriving at Lancaster from Philadelphia on the turnpike, pioneers headed northwest on an unimproved dirt road to the Susquehanna River (See Figure 5). Apart from drovers driving livestock, most people chose to cross the wide river on a ferry, if one was available. Although there were several ferry crossing along the length of the Susquehanna, the most used ferries for pioneers heading to the western part of the state from Philadelphia were Harris' Ferry at what later became the city of Harrisburg and the ferries at the junction of the Susquehanna and Juniata Rivers.

John Harris established Harris' ferry at his trading post in 1733.[23] It was about thirty-five miles northwest of Lancaster. About eighteen miles upriver from Harris' Ferry were the ferries at the junction of the Susquehanna and Juniata Rivers.

For travelers heading west to Pittsburgh and beyond, these two crossings were used more than others. They led to unimproved dirt roads, formerly Indian trails, that traveled through valleys, rather than over

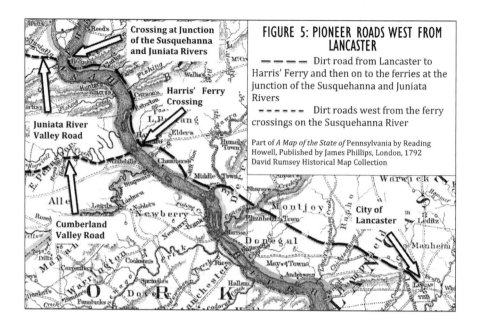

FIGURE 5: PIONEER ROADS WEST FROM LANCASTER

— — — — Dirt road from Lancaster to Harris' Ferry and then on to the ferries at the junction of the Susquehanna and Juniata Rivers

- - - - - Dirt roads west from the ferry crossings on the Susquehanna River

Part of *A Map of the State of* Pennsylvania by Reading Howell, Published by James Phillips, London, 1792 David Rumsey Historical Map Collection

Crossing at Junction of the Susquehanna and Juniata Rivers

Harris' Ferry Crossing

Juniata River Valley Road

Cumberland Valley Road

mountains. Having crossed on Harris' Ferry, pioneers could choose from dirt roads that took them southwest through Cumberland Valley. While taking one of the ferries that crossed at the junction of the Susquehanna and Juniata Rivers, travelers could take unimproved dirt roads that went northwest through the Juniata River Valley. As pioneers crossed the Susquehanna on one of these ferries, they likely carried their belongings westward in a Conestoga Wagon (See Figure 6).[24]

Conestoga wagons evolved in the early 18th century in Lancaster County, Pennsylvania. They were developed to carry farm products from Lancaster County to Philadelphia and then carry needed commodities from Philadelphia back to the farmers. The name Conestoga comes from the Conestoga Valley in Lancaster, where the wagon may have first developed.[25]

Since the wagons were designed for carrying freight, they were especially useful in carrying pioneers' possessions. They were the moving vans of their day. The beds of wagons were about 16 feet long and 4 feet wide. Their beds sloped upward from the middle towards each end, giving the wagons a boat-like shape. The shape of the wagons helped the

FIGURE 6: NEWBOLD HOUGH TROTTER, CONESTOGA WAGON
(Courtesy of the Pennsylvania State Museum)

pioneers' possessions from slipping when the wagons went up or down steep inclines. Above the wagons' beds were from 6 to 13 hoops over which a white canopy made of canvas was placed. The Conestoga was very colorful with its body painted Prussian blue, its running gear and sides painted red and its white cloth canopies. The wagons themselves weighed between three thousand and thirty-five hundred pounds and could carry several thousand pounds of cargo.[26]

Because of the heavy weight of the wagon plus its cargo, it had to be pulled by from four to six strong draft animals, usually Conestoga horses. The horses stood about five feet high at their shoulders and weighed about eighteen hundred pounds.[27] Benjamin Long does not mention in the previously described narrative what type of wagons and horses the Long family used, but they were likely Conestoga.

No information was found on the cost of crossing the Susquehanna with a Conestoga at either Harris' Ferry or one of the ferries at the junction of the Susquehanna and Juniata Rivers. However, in 1787, the year before John and his son Daniel started their ferry, an article was published in the *Pennsylvania Chronicle* that Anderson's Ferry had "lowered the price of the ferriage of a four-horse wagon to three shillings and ninepence, and that of a man and horse to sixpence, and all other things in proportion."[28] Anderson's Ferry was located down the Susquehanna River from Harris' Ferry at the town of Marietta.

SERVING UP A *WEE DRAM* (A SHOT OF WHISKEY)

As previously discussed, John Clark had purchased the property for Clark's Tavern and Ferry Landing in 1787. Around 1788, he and his son Daniel had moved onto the property and started their ferry business. The exact year when their tavern was started is not known. When John bought the property from Samuel Goudy and his wife, Sarah, we know from his "Valuable Plantation To Be Sold" advertisement that it had "two small dwelling houses," probably made of log.[29] A tradition of the Smith family, who lived in the tavern from *c.* 1880 until 1974, says that the earliest part of the tavern was a log house.[30]

Samuel Goudy's earliest log structure was probably a crudely constructed log cabin with rounded logs and saddle notches. By the time John Clark bought the property twenty-one years later, it is likely that at least one of his two structures was a well-constructed log house. It would have been made of hewn flat logs with interlocking corner notches.[31] The Clarks likely used one of the Goudys' log houses as a rudimentary tavern.

Today, a tavern is thought of as an establishment where alcoholic and other beverages are served along with food. During the 18th and into the 19th century, most taverns or as they were also called public houses, houses of public entertainment, ordinaries or inns, provided food and drink as well as other services such as lodging.[32] The services provided depended upon where the tavern was located and what types of customers it served.[33] Was it an urban or rural tavern? What were the livelihoods, social positions, and economical means of its customers?

Taverns, by definition, sold alcoholic beverages. Because they sold alcohol, they were required by law to have a license. There is no known Clark's tavern license application until 1790, two years after Clark's Ferry service started. In 1790, Cumberland County recommended Daniel Clark for a tavern license.[34] He may have been recommended before this date, but no records have been found. Without a license, Clark's Tavern would have been considered an illegal tavern known as a tippling house. Tippling houses were common at the time. It was often less expensive to pay a fine for running an illegal tavern than it was for paying a fee for a tavern license.[35]

Another clue to the starting date of Clark's Tavern can be found in a 1793 road petition. In the petition, it stated that Daniel Clark ". . . has for some years past established a ferry on the Susquehanna a short distance from the mouth of the Juniata." It goes on to say, "he . . . also provides for the accommodation of travelers," i.e., has a tavern.[36]

This statement is informative because it not only gives an approximate date for the start of the tavern, but it describes Daniel as overseeing both the tavern and the ferry.

The next mention of Daniel running the tavern is in a Cumberland County Tavern License Recommendation for 1794. What happened to his recommendations for the years 1791–1793 is not known.[37] Tavern recommendations for 1795 and 1796 are also missing. Tavern license recommendations continue for Daniel in 1797 and 1798. In 1799, Daniel's younger brother, Robert, not Daniel, was recommended for the tavern license.[38] It thus appears that in addition to running John Clark's Ferry service for about ten years, Daniel Clark was also in charge of Clark's Tavern during that time.

Whether legally or illegally, it is likely the Clark family sold alcoholic beverages and prepared food for travelers from early-on. Travelers waiting for a ferry to the Dauphin County side of the river or those who had just arrived would have expected an opportunity to purchase food and alcoholic beverages from the tavern. During that period, most immigrants from Europe considered alcoholic beverages a necessity of life. Even though the water outside of cities in America was drinkable, water in American and European cities was not because of contamination. As a result, drinking alcoholic beverages was a custom for European settlers. Not only did immigrating Europeans drink alcohol to quench their thirst, but they also drank it for enjoyment, to aid digestion, keep warm, increase strength, and cure whatever ailed them.[39]

As previously mentioned, when John Clark bought the Goudy property, it had "about 100 bearing apple trees" on it.[40] The apples from the orchard, along with the apple mill and press, a hogshead, barrels, and casks (all listed in John Clark's estate inventory), give evidence that the Clarks made cider from their apples.[41] After making cider, it was a simple process to turn it first into hard cider and then into applejack.

To make hard cider, all the Clarks needed to do was to put the cider in barrels and let it sit. After a time, the natural sugars in the cider would ferment, giving it a low alcoholic content. The alcoholic content of apple cider is about five percent. Because it was easy and cheap to make, more of it was likely drunk in America at that time than any other alcoholic beverage. The average American drank an estimated 15 gallons a year.[42] To further strengthen the alcoholic content of the beverage, the Clarks needed to turn the hard cider into applejack. This would have been done using a freeze distillation method.

To make applejack, the Clarks would have set barrels of hard cider outside to freeze during the winter. Freezing temperatures would have caused the water in the cider to float to the top and freeze into ice. While the water was freezing, the alcohol in the cider would sink unfrozen to the bottom. Ice from the top of the cider would then be removed, leaving a more alcoholic beverage beneath it. After repeating this process several times throughout the winter, the result was a beverage called applejack. Its alcoholic content could be as high as thirty percent.[43]

Based on John Clark's 1800 Estate Inventory, another alcoholic beverage was likely being made at or near the tavern, whiskey.[44] Since the Clark's were from Scotland, whiskey was likely one of the major alcoholic beverages they served.

By the 18th century, whiskey had become a fundamental part of Scottish life. It was considered a stimulant during Scotland's cold and lengthy winters as well as a medicinal cure. In addition, it became a mandatory custom to offer guests a "wee dram" upon their arrival.[45] As previously discussed, this is what brought about David Long's fortunate delay when crossing the Susquehanna River in 1814.

John Clark's 1800 estate inventory listed him having 11½ acres of rye in the fields and 26 bushels in storage.[46] Rye whiskey was the prevalent type of whiskey in Pennsylvania in the late 1700s and early 1800s.[47] About 2 gallons of rye whiskey can be distilled from one bushel of rye.[48] Therefore, the 26 bushels of rye in storage at Clark's would have produced about 52 gallons of whiskey.

Today, it takes .6277 acres of rye to produce a bushel of rye grain. Making allowances for improvements in agricultural methods over the last two hundred years, we might estimate that it took .75 acres to produce one bushel of rye in 1800. As such, in addition to the rye grain in storage, the Clarks 11½ acres of rye would have produced an additional 8.625 bushels of rye. This, in turn, could have been distilled into about 17 gallons of whiskey. Combining the amount of rye grain in storage with that still in the field, the Clarks could have made about 69 gallons of rye whiskey from their rye grain once harvested. This would have been enough to quench the thirst of any good Scotsman.

We do not know if John Clark distilled his own whiskey. No distillation equipment is listed in his estate inventory, nor was any found in the 2012–2015 archaeological excavation of the tavern site. It is likely he had a business arrangement with Mathias Flam to distill his whiskey. In 1786, the year before John Clark bought Silver Spring from Samuel Goudy and his wife, tax records for the township show Mathias and his brother, Henry Flam, taxed for two stills.[49] When Robert Clark bought Mathias Flam's Landing in Dauphin County in 1804, Flam had a distillery on it.[50] It was customary at the time for a distiller to receive one-half of the alcohol he distilled.[51]

Although no historical or archaeological evidence has been uncovered, another alcoholic beverage was probably made by the Clarks or Mathias Flam and served at the tavern, ale. In Scotland, ale was brewed in many households and served at most meals.[52] In Scotland, it was brewed from oats and heather. In America, ale would have been made using available ingredients. It was drunk more to quench your thirst than for taste.[53]

During the late 18th century, rum in America became the most popular drink until whiskey took its place in the early 1800s. Although not made by the Clarks, it was undoubtedly served in their tavern. Its popularity declined after 1808. During that year, the United States Government passed a law ending the slave trade into the United States. When the law was passed, it effectively broke the "triangle trade" between

Africa, the West Indies, and the United States. This made rum and the molasses it was made from less available and, therefore, more expensive. Whiskey stepped in to fill the void.[54]

Alcoholic beverages were licensed to be served at Clark's Tavern by members of the Clark family as early as 1790. From 1790, when the tavern was first licensed, until 1788, the Clark's oldest son, Daniel, was licensed to operate Clark's Tavern.[55] In 1789, Daniel's younger brother Robert was licensed to run the tavern for the first time. He continued to be licensed in 1800, 1801, and 1802. From 1803 until 1810, however, no petitions for Clark's Tavern were uncovered. These lost petitions likely belonged to Robert as he again petitioned to run the tavern in 1810. No tavern petition was uncovered for 1811, but Robert again petitioned to run the tavern in 1812 and 1813. After 1813, no further tavern license petitions were uncovered for a member of the Clark family .[56]

During the years 1814 and 1815, tavern license petitions to run Clark's Tavern were found for Joseph Robison. Throughout four months of these two years, Robert was away serving in the Pennsylvania Militia during the War of 1812. Although in 1816, Robert Clark was back from his military service, Robert Patton was licensed to run the tavern. No tavern petitions were found for the years 1817 and 1818.[57]

In H.H. Hain's *History of Perry County* and Franklin Ellis' *History of that Part of the Susquehanna . . .* , the historians stated that John Boden and then Henry Lemon ran the tavern. [58] No record was found for Henry Lemon, but a Henry Leman/Leyman petitioned to run a tavern in Cumberland County in 1819 and 1820. The record does not mention the name of the tavern, but it was possibly Clark's.[59] Hain also stated that William Wilson "kept the tavern" after Boden.[60] To date, no record has been found for William Wilson keeping a tavern in Cumberland or Perry Counties.

After Perry County was created from Cumberland County in 1820, the next record we have of a tavern license for Clark's Tavern was in 1827. That year, Robert Clark placed an advertisement in the *Oracle of Dauphin* newspaper. In it, he states that his brother-in-law, John Boden, "occupied" the tavern, i.e., indicated that he ran it.[61] Perry County Township Taxes also showed John Boden running a tavern in 1829 and 1830, presumably Clark's.[62]

According to township tax records, after John Boden, the next recorded innkeeper at Clark's Tavern, was Benjamin E. Roney in 1835.
Originally in Rye Township, Clark's Tavern was in Wheatfield Township
by that time. Township records from 1838 mention three innkeepers,
but do not mention the names of their taverns. The innkeepers were
Cornelius Baskins, John Cougher, and John Keiser. Of these, the most
likely to have been Clark's innkeeper was John Keiser. Silas Wright, in his
History of Perry County, mentions that John Keiser kept the post office at
Clark's Ferry.[63] Keiser was again taxed as an innkeeper in 1842.[64]

By 1840, Clark's Tavern was in Penn Township. The first tavern license found In Penn Township for Clark's Tavern was in 1844. That year
and in 1845, 1847, and 1850 Robert McCoy was taxed as the tavern/
innkeeper at Clark's Tavern.[65]

In Penn Township, no tavern taxes were found again until 1853. That
year, three men were mentioned as tavern/innkeepers, John B. Topley,
Samuel Mc Kinzie, and Cornelius Baskins. Although the names of their
taverns were not given, Topley was running a tavern in Petersburg and
Baskins, no doubt, at Baskin's Ferry Landing. That leaves Samuel Mc
Kinzie as the keeper for Clark's Tavern.[66] After 1853, tavern/innkeepers
were no longer taxed as an occupation in Perry County.

Oral tradition has it that Clark's Tavern eventually became the Topley
Hotel. This tradition is not substantiated by Perry County tax records
or tavern license applications. Although John B. Topley is listed in the
tax records as a tavern/innkeeper in 1842, 1844, 1845, 1847, 1850, and
1853, it was not at Clark's Tavern. Instead, he apparently ran one and
sometimes two inns/hotels in Petersburg. One of these was at Cougher's
House.[67] It is not known if Topley leased Clark's Tavern as a hotel from
Robert or Margaretta after 1853.

A UNGIRIE MAN SUN SNIFFS OUT MEAT
(A HUNGRY MAN WILL SOON FIND FOOD)

Besides selling guests alcoholic beverages, having come from Scotland, it
is likely Clark's tavern made and served simply prepared Scottish food.

The tavern's meals and drinks would have been served on the first floor of the tavern. The first floor was likely to have had only one room. It would have been the public room or bar room where most activities except sleeping took place. The room would have contained a walk-in fireplace for cooking, a bar for serving drinks, and at least one table and several chairs.

A bar today refers to a counter on which drinks are served. In the 18th century, a bar would have been a counter, but the counter would have been part of a wooden cage or closet, i.e., a bar cage. The bar cage or closet would have had a gate or grate above the counter with bars. The gate would be opened when serving, but closed when not, thus sealing off the alcoholic contents behind it. In John Lewis Krimmel's painting, *Interior of an American Inn*, a bar cage can be seen in the background with a table and chairs in the foreground (See Figure 7).[68]

In one part of John Clark's 1800 estate inventory, it lists "a bar." In addition, it lists other items needed to cook for and serve both Clark family members and tavern customers. Bar or public room items listed

FIGURE 7: JOHN LEWIS KRIMMEL, "INTERIOR OF AN AMERICAN INN," 1823
(Courtesy of the Toledo Museum of Art)

were a dough tray, a dresser (hutch), one old walnut table, cooking utensils, cupboards, and chairs. In addition, the inventory listed table settings of "China Delft & Queens Ware."[69] It must be remembered that this inventory was taken in 1800, approximately ten years after the tavern was first established. It is unlikely that when the tavern first started, c. 1790, travelers and members of the Clark family would have eaten off refined earthenware such as Delft and Queens Ware. Given the pioneer conditions of the tavern at its start, it is more likely dinnerware was redware or was made of wood or pewter.

Food in rural frontier taverns like John Clark's would have been mediocre at best. People ate because they were hungry, not because the food was appetizing. Travelers would have been served whatever the Clark family was eating.[70] Since the Clark's were from Scotland, their Scottish food was likely to have had "severe plainness in cooking and monotony in fair."[71]

During the early years of the tavern, meat was probably rarely served. John Clark's county tax assessment in 1788 listed only two horses and four cows.[72] The cows were probably used for milk products. In 1789, the year after they settled, John is taxed for only three cows.[73] It is possible that after the tax was taken in August of the previous year, one of the cows was slaughtered. It was a custom in Scotland to kill beef in the fall and salt it, so a family would have meat throughout the winter.[74]

As for cultivated plants, as Scots, John Clark and his family likely grew kale, oatmeal, barley, turnips, onions, and potatoes for their own consumption as well as for the consumption of travelers. These were staple ingredients in the diet of ordinary Scotsmen in the 18th century.[75]

Before the start of Scotland's agricultural revolution in 1790, Scottish food for farmers and workers "was monotonously poor, for they had nothing to eat except the everlasting oatmeal and "knockit bere," and "kail greens . . ."[76] "Knockit bere" was a broth made of barley with leftover bones of fowl. Sometimes leftover kail or peas were also added.[77] Except for kale, turnips ("neaps"), and potatoes, vegetables were lacking in their diet. Turnips were occasionally served as dessert.[78]

Wheat bread was not likely to have been served during the early years of the tavern. Because of the cold, damp climate and poor soil of Scotland, wheat was difficult to grow and expensive. In Scotland, wheat bread could only be afforded by the wealthy.[79]

Instead of wheat bread, oatmeal or barley bannocks were likely served at Clark's Tavern. A bannock is unleavened, round flatbread, cut into quarters called scones. It is usually cooked on a flat griddle.[80] Bannocks could be made of oats or barley. Sometimes oats and barley were mixed.[81]

In his book, *The Social Life of Scotland*, Henky Grey Graham describes the typical meals served in Scotland in the 18th century. Probably something like this fare was served to both family members and travelers at the start of Clark's Tavern.

- For breakfast, "oatmeal porridge with milk or ale, or broth made of cabbage left overnight, and oat bannock."
- For dinner, you might have had "sowans, with milk and oat-cakes or kail." Sowans is a dish made from the husks of oats after milling. The husks are placed in water and allowed to ferment. After a few days or a week, liquor forms on the surface. It can be skimmed off and drunk. The husks at the bottom of the fermented liquid are known as sowans. They were boiled with salt and water until forming a porridge. The flavor of the porridge is sour but could be served dipped into milk or with cream or butter.
- For supper, kail (leaf cabbage), with oat-cakes.[82]

Perhaps by today's standards, there was one appetizing meal served at Clark's Tavern in its early years, fish. Much of Scotland is not far from the coast, a loch, or one of its many rivers. Being ferrymen and living next to the Susquehanna River and Clark's Run, fish was probably served at Clark's Tavern on a regular basis. In Cumberland County during the early years of Clark's Tavern, "The streams, unpolluted . . . were alive with fish, principally bass, pike and trout. After severe winters shad, rockfish, salmon and perch ascended the streams . . ."[83] Of these, the most sought after and eaten by the Clarks was likely salmon. In Scotland in the 18th century, like today, Salmon was abundant in all its rivers.[84]

By 1800, ten years after John and his son, Daniel, started their tavern, food at the tavern was more varied. Township taxes show the Clark family having at their tavern the following eatable livestock:

- 3 cows (1 red and white, 1 flecked and 1 black)
- 1 yearling heifer
- 15 sheep and 3 lambs
- 12 head of swine
- 9 small pigs.[85]

Being from Scotland, the addition of sheep over time to the tavern's collection of livestock is to be expected. Sheep had long been raised in Scotland. In Scotland, however, sheep were primarily raised for their wool. They were never eaten unless they were found dead of hunger, disease, or old age.[86] When the Scots ate their succumbed sheep, they did not waste any of it. Mrs. Frazer in her 1791 Scottish cookbook describes several ways the Clarks might have prepared and served their deceased sheep.[87] The following are two of her recipes:

- **Haggis** – Made from meat that was thrown away in many countries was a large sausage casing made from a sheep's stomach. In it would usually be placed a mixture of minced sheep's lungs, liver, and heart along with oatmeal, suet, onions, and spices.[88] Boil the bag and its contents for at least two hours.

- **A Pudding of Sheep's Blood or Black Pudding** – Break all the clots of the blood of a sheep. Run it through a sieve. Mix in new milk according to the quantity of blood. Season it with salt pepper, onions, and mint. Cut a sheep's suet into small pieces. Mix all the ingredients along with oatmeal into cleaned intestines and tie the ends together. Place the skins in boiling water. "When they are in a while, prick them with a pin to let out the wind."[89]

In addition to sheep, by 1800, the Clark family owned 12 head of swine and 9 small pigs. With this number of swine, pork must have been regularly served at the tavern. Unlike sheep, however, Scotsmen did not generally eat pork. In Scotland, "though pork was sometimes presented at table, few ate of it when fresh, and even when cured it was not generally acceptable."[90] Mrs. Frazer, in her 1791 cookbook, however, did describe a recipe for cooking pork that might have been served in 1800 at Clark's Tavern.

- **Roasted Leg of Pork** – Skewer the leg after you score the leg and stuff the knuckle with sage and onion. While roasting, pour a mixture of gravy and applesauce over the leg. Turn quickly while roasting before a strong fire.[91]

Most other pork dishes served at the tavern must have been adopted from neighbors and visitors from locations other than Scotland.

In 1800, with only three cows and one yearling heifer, tavern guests must have been served beef only occasionally at the tavern. From John Clark's one heifer, veil could have been made from one of Mrs. Frazer's 18th-century roasting or boiling recipes.[92]

In addition to improved food at the tavern, lodging accommodations improved over time. By 1798, when the U.S. Direct Tax was taken, the first stone addition had been added onto the original log structure. The exact date when the first stone addition was added to the log structure is not certain. The stone part of the building could have been started the same year as the ferry, 1788. It is not likely, however, that the timber frame part of the building was started before 1789, the following year. Examination by the author of the timber framing and boards in the earliest stone part of the tavern shows its lumber has vertical water-sawn marks. This indicates the framing and boards were cut with a water-powered reciprocating saw. The earliest known reciprocating sawmill in the area that could have cut the wooden components for the tavern was Hartman's. Nicholas Wolf and his son-in-law John Bowman built this sawmill in 1789.[93] If Hartman's Sawmill was not built until 1789, the wooden parts of the tavern were not likely to have been built until the following year, 1790.

Today, the first floor of the tavern's first stone addition has the same layout as it did in 1800. On the first floor of the first stone addition, are two rooms, a stair hall, and a main hall. The main hall would have been a multifunctional room for eating and other get-togethers. It contained about twice the square footage of the bar or pub room in the original log tavern. Cooking would not have been done in the main hall, however, because the fireplace in the hall was built only for warmth, not cooking. Meals would have continued to have been prepared in the bar or pub room in the log part of the tavern. With the new c.1790 stone addition, larger numbers of people could have "dined in spacious comfort" in the main hall.[94]

Most of the dining room furniture and serving pieces listed in John Clark's 1800 Estate Inventory were likely to have been used in the main hall. They included the following: 1 dining table, 1 mahogany breakfast table, 1 walnut breakfast table, and 18 Windsor chairs." The previously mentioned "China Delf & Queens Ware" would have been in use in the main hall by 1800 along with "1 Half Dozen Silver Tea Spoons & Silver Tea Tongs, 4 Servers & Knives and Forks and Brass Candlesticks."[95]

Because of increased westward migration from 1787 to 1800, the tavern building not only needed to be expanded, but the facilities outside the tavern needed expanded as well. From the 1798 Tax, we know that by that date, John Clark had built a 68' x 26' barn for storage.[96] The tax did not describe how and of what material the barn was constructed. Given that all the structures at the tavern site, except the stone tavern building itself, were swept away in an 1865 flood, it is likely the barn was made of wood, probably log.[97]

With ever-increasing wagon traffic, after the opening of the Philadelphia to Lancaster Turnpike in 1794, there would have been a need for a large wagon yard at the tavern. Although not giving any sources, Hain, in his *History of Perry County* states that "In the old inn-yard could be seen often a dozen or more of the wagons, drawn by six or eight horses, which were being fed while awaiting their turn to be ferried."[98] The 1798

Tax described the size of the tavern lot as one acre, twenty-four perches.[99] Because the Susquehanna River was on the North Market street side of the building, Clark's Run on the Clark Street side, and a hill on the Apple Tree Alley side, the location of the tavern's wagon yard was likely on the Margaretta Street side of the building.

In addition to the tavern being a place of respite for travelers, the local male population would have gathered there. Male members of the community would have come together at the tavern to gossip about people and events, discuss politics or business, obtain information from newspapers, and pick up the mail.[100]

Until 1798, the mail was delivered to the tavern on random days by postal riders on horseback. In 1798, Postmaster General Joseph Habersham set up scheduled mail delivery, which stopped at Clark's Tavern. On October 15th of that year, until April 15th, a post rider left Harrisburg "every other Monday at 6 o'clock A.M., returning the next Monday by 7 P.M., other seasons of the year in proportion to days' length."[101] When the post rider arrived with the mail at the tavern, he likely just placed the mail on one of the tavern's table for anyone to pick up and read.[102]

BEDS ARE BEST, QUOTH THE GOOD MAN TO THE GUEST (AN INVITATION TO SLEEP IN A BED)

Regarding the other major function of a tavern, i.e., lodging, it is unlikely beds were available for early travelers because of the small size of the original log tavern. Perhaps in bad weather, a sleeping spot would have been offered to travelers on the floor in front of the fireplace.

After the first stone addition was added to the log building, c.1790, some lodging for travelers could have been offered. The new addition contained two rooms above the main hall that would have served as bedrooms. Although crowded at times, these two rooms, along with one or two rooms on the second floor of the log portion of the tavern, would have allowed sleeping quarters for both Clark family members and some travelers.

In rural taverns of that time, the usual number of beds for travelers was from six to eight.[103] Accounting for two people to a bed, this number of beds could sleep up to sixteen people. These guests were usually men. Women rarely stayed at frontier taverns before the development of turnpikes and the arrival of stagecoaches and carriages.

In John Clark's 1800 Estate Inventory, it listed the tavern having six beds:

- one chaff bead and bedding and bedstead
- one feather bed and bedding and bedstead
- four feather beds and bedding and bedsteads with curtains.[104]

This number seems to fall within the usual six to eight-bed average needed for a tavern. A problem with the number arises; however, when the number of Clark family members is factored into the equation. The 1800 U.S. Census lists 10 Clark family members living at the tavern at that time.[105] If Clark family members slept two to a bed, this would have allowed only one bed for two guests. Perhaps if there were more paying guests than beds, family members would have been required to triple-up in a bed or sleep on the floor.

The types of beds listed in the inventory are interesting. Whoever had to sleep on the chaff bed must have been considered the least important or lowest in rank, i.e., likely the youngest children. When guests purchased the use of a bed for the night, they were likely given the feather beds with curtains. The curtains on four of the beds would have provided guests additional privacy and warmth.[106]

DEATH AT ONE DOOR

On April 19, 1794, the patriarch of the Clark family, John Clark, died.[107] The cause and location of his death are not known. There was likely a notice of his death placed in Harrisburg's newspaper, the *Oracle of Dauphin*, but the issues around the date of John's death are missing.

Unfortunately, the burial location of John Clark as well as his wife, Margaret, their oldest son Daniel, and their second-oldest son John is not known. Given that there is no known Clark family graveyard, early Clark family members could have been buried at nearby Baskin's family graveyard, but this seems unlikely. The Baskin family had a graveyard on a bluff above their ferry landing about one-half mile up the Susquehanna River from Clarks Tavern. More than likely, early members of the Clark family were interred at Dick's Gap Presbyterian Church Cemetery.

Established c. 1766, Dick's Gap Presbyterian Church was one of the first churches established in what is Perry County today. It was located in what is today Miller Township.[108] The church was abandoned and replaced by Middle Ridge Church in 1803.[109] Although known to have been located in Miller Township, the exact location of the church and its cemetery are not known.[110] Unfortunately, there are also no known written records remaining of the church or its cemetery.

Both before and for four years after John Clark's death in 1794, Clark's Ferry and Tavern were run by John and Margaret's oldest son, Daniel. As previously mentioned, Daniel was recommended for the tavern's license as early as 1790.[111] He was licensed to run Clark's Tavern until 1799.[112]

Other Clark family members likely helped to make Clark's Ferry, Tavern, and farm function. Regrettably, nothing has been uncovered about their contributions. John's wife, Margaret, would have played an essential role in raising the Clark children and helping to run the businesses. At the time of John's death, John and Margaret's adult children must have also done their part in keeping the businesses running. At the time of John's death, the adult children were Daniel, Catherine John (Robert's elder brother), Robert and Christina. At the time of his death, he and Margaret also had three younger children under 10 years of age. They were Jane, Ann (sometimes called Nancy) and Peter.[113]

After John Clark's death, for reasons unknown, his estate was not settled for seven years. Taxes like the U.S. Direct Tax ("glass tax") of 1798 were still in his name.[114]

When John died, the Clark enterprises consisted of a ferry, tavern, and farm. They continued to be run under Daniel's supervision until 1799. That year, Daniel's second youngest brother, Robert, was issued a tavern's license for the first time.[115] Although Daniel likely continued to have a part in running the ferry, Robert rather than Daniel was taxed in Dauphin County for a ferry that year. This administrative takeover by Robert may have reflected Daniel becoming ill and unable to fulfill his ferry responsibilities as he died in September of the following year, 1800.[116]

Daniel's possible incapacity is also reflected in the administration of John Clark's estate. As the eldest son, Daniel would have been expected to be appointed to administer his father's estate. He was not. On April 8, 1800, Robert, not Daniel, was appointed to administer John Clark's estate.[117] On May 7, 1800, Robert, began administrating John's estate by conducting a two-page estate inventory of his father's personal holdings.[118]

Four months later, on Wednesday, September 17, 1800, Daniel Clark died. The notice of his death was found in two newspapers, Carlisle's *Kline's Gazette* and Harrisburg's *Oracle of Dauphin*. Strangely, Daniel's previously described newspaper dispute with Samuel Ellis and Mathias Flam occurred only about two months before his death.

On September 22, 1800, five days after Daniel's death, the following notice of death was placed in the *Oracle of Dauphin*.

> Died on Wednesday last, about 12 o'clock at noon, after a short
> illness and in the prime of life, Mr. Daniel Clark, the eldest son
> of the late John Clark, deceased. He was an industrious, obliging,
> and kindhearted young man.[119]

Two days after the *Oracle's* notice, Carlisle's *Kline's Gazette* placed a shorter notice about his death on September 24th.

> Died on Wednesday last at the mouth of the Juniata, Mr. Daniel
> Clark, the eldest son of the late John Clark, deceased.[120]

The nature of his "short illness" is not known, but as a ferryman, he would have been constantly exposed to people carrying contagious diseases. As settlers moved west from cities like Philadelphia and Lancaster, they carried all manner of contagious diseases with them. In the 18th century, Philadelphia was a breeding ground for diseases experiencing sixty-six epidemics. Among the contagious diseases being passed around in Philadelphia were eleven epidemics of scarlet fever, thirteen of smallpox, nine respiratory illnesses, six of measles, two of typhoid, and three of typhus. There were also six unclassified diseases.[121] As people moved westward from Philadelphia, Daniel and other ferrymen would have been continuously exposed to many of these diseases. It is also possible that Daniel made a trip to Philadelphia, where he contracted a noncontagious disease such as yellow fever. The fever struck Philadelphia eight times between 1793 and 1805.[122] Unfortunately, like his father, the burial place of Daniel is not known.

By the time Daniel died in 1800, the Clark family had become successful businessmen owning ferry, tavern, and farm businesses. When the 1798 U.S. Direct Tax was taken two years earlier, the total value of the family's businesses, excluding the worth of their land and buildings, was 313 pounds.[123] This included the value of the ferry, tavern and farm's equipment as well as the tavern's furnishing and farm animals. Of the 313 pounds, it was calculated by the author that about 24% of the money was invested in ferrying, 30% in the running the tavern, and 46 % in farming.[124] In regards to their ferry business, when John Clark's estate inventory was taken, it listed two large flats or ferryboats in service (See Figure 8).

In addition, the inventory listed one smaller ferryboat "not finished," along with "2 old canoes."[125] The two larger flats (because they had flat bottoms), would have been the ones referred to in Daniel Clark's earlier newspaper reply to Francis Ellis in the *Oracle of Dauphin*. The fact that the Clarks were constructing a flat-bottomed ferryboat at the time of Daniel's death indicates they may have brought boat-building skills with them from Scotland. The types of flats or ferryboats they used had a barge design. Ferryboats or barges had been built for crossing rivers in Great Britain since medieval times.

Despite all his endeavors and his importance to Clark's businesses, Daniel Clark had few material possessions when he died on September 17, 1800. On December 4, 1800, Robert Clark was appointed to administer Daniel's estate.[126] When Daniel's estate was inventoried on March 5, 1801, it recorded that Daniel had only one horse with a saddle and bridle and one "smooth bore gun." Together their combined value was listed at forty-two pounds and ten shillings. In addition, Daniel's inventory listed

FIGURE 8: MODEL OF A FLAT-BOTTOMED FERRY CARRYING A CONESTOGA WAGON
Part of Diorama at the National Road & Zane Gray Museum, Norwich, Ohio (Courtesy of Richard Hopper)

ten pounds cash as well as a note from ferryman Mitchel Baskin for one pound, a "book out" (debt) against Mathias Flam for eleven pounds, fourpence, and seven shillings and another one for Robert Armstrong for eight pounds and eight shillings. In the inventory, it stated Daniel still had "A lease of a ferry House and Privilege of landing from Mathias Flam . . ."[127] This indicates that by 1800, the Clarks had not yet set up their own ferry landing on the Dauphin County side of the Susquehanna.

Although the Clarks were still leasing Mathias Flam's Landing in 1800 when Daniel died, it appears that Robert Clark had already started the process of preparing to establish his own landing on the Dauphin County side of the river. In Mathias Flam's previously described July 12, 1800 newspaper notice, Flam stated, "Tis True his brother Robert has lately purchased a few acres on the end of Peter's Mountain, near Foster's Falls."[128] This would have been adjacent to and just south of Mathias Flam's 50 acres. When, however, the 1800 taxes were taken in Upper Paxton Township, Dauphin County, Robert was taxed for a ferry, but nothing else.[129]

3

Peak Ferry and Tavern Period
(1802–1836)

Robert Takes Possession of Clark's Enterprises

I n 1801, Robert Clark began to take command and expand Clark's businesses. On July 22nd of that year, Robert negotiated an agreement with Mathias Flam to buy in installments Flam's Landing and its 50 acres.[1]

In the sales agreement, Robert Clark and Mathias Flam agreed that on or before August 10, 1801, the property would be conveyed to Robert under the following conditions:

- Robert would pay Mathias 100 pounds on August 10th.
- He would pay Mathias 200 more pounds on May 15th of the following year
- On completion of payment, Robert would take full possession of the houses, barns, and all the premises.
- Robert was to pay Flam yearly 100 pounds on the 1st day of May until his debt for the property was paid.

In the meantime, until payment was completed, the following would be in effect:

- Robert "is to get possession of the new Stone House with the privilege of all the landing on the first day of August next . . ."

This building was to become Robert's Lower Ferry tavern building, which he leased out.

- "All suits against each of the parties by the other Respecting the lands, Rents, Rights of titles shall be discontinued." These lawsuits likely resulted from the previously discussed debts owed at the time of Daniel Clark's death.
- "Robert Clark Shall be exonerated from paying, and Rents or any part of the expenses for the building of the new [stone] house as was agreed on in a certain article between M. Flam and Dan'l Clark deceased."
- "Mathias Flam reserves the house he now lived in with the Barn's Stabling & still house to the fifteenth of May next."

Robert paid off and took complete ownership of Mathias Flam's Landing on November 5, 1804.[2]

On the Cumberland County side of the Susquehanna, in August of 1801, Robert applied for and received a license for Clark's Tavern. In his application, he stated that the tavern would be "in the house now occupied by him as a tavern."[3]

In 1802, death once again came knocking at the Clark family door. Although no death notices were found, it is likely the matriarch of the family, Margaret, died sometime early that year. Later in 1802, Robert applied for and received guardianship for the family's youngest children. They were Ann (called Nancy in the appointment document), Jane and Peter. At that time, all were under the age of fourteen.[4]

In addition, around the same time, Robert petitioned the Cumberland County Court to conduct an inquest into the feasibility of dividing the family's 215 acres equally without "spoiling the whole." The acreage was to be divided among the deceased John and Margaret Clark's seven children; Catherine, John, Christina, Robert, Ann, Jane, and Peter.[5]

Shortly after Robert's petition to the court, on Sunday, August 22, 1802, the Clarks' second eldest son, John (Robert's elder brother) died.[6] The role John played in the Clark family is a mystery. Being the second-born son after Daniel, he should have had important responsibilities in helping to run the family businesses, but none were found. Only one description of him was found. In the 1800 Septennial Census, it describes his vocation as "Capt.," i.e., Captain (See Figure 9).[7] The title captain seems to indicate he served in the military, but no mention of him was found in military service records from that period. The title may have been an honorary name given to him for running the tavern while Daniel primarily ran the ferry and Robert surveyed.

In 1799, the year before his death, Robert's elder brother, John, was the likely successor to have run both the ferry and tavern. That year, however, John's younger brother, Robert, took charge of both enterprises. The following year, 1800, Robert Clark, rather than, John was appointed to administer both their father's and Daniel's estate. Like his father, mother and elder brother, Daniel, the location of John's burial is not known, but was likely Dick's Gap Presbyterian Cemetery.

In September of 1802, Robert wrote a curious letter to Cumberland County Court Judge, James Hamilton. The letter was regarding a visit paid to the Clarks' property by the county sheriff. In his letter, Robert expressed surprise that one of his neighbors, Mr. Jones, would have suggested to the sheriff that he "have a view on Clarks Place." A view would have been an inspection of the property. In Robert's letter he stated that the sheriff "had no orders yet and that he did not know anything concerning it." Robert goes on to ask Judge Hamilton that if the sheriff were to be given orders to investigate the Clarks' property, "I wish it be done before the court." The outcome of Robert's request to the court was not found.[8]

On October 10, 1802, one month after Robert's letter to Judge Hamilton, the Cumberland County Court gave a reply to Robert's earlier request to equally divide the Clarks' property among the surviving Clark children "without injury to and spoiling the whole." Since John (the second oldest son) had died the previous August, the division was to be between the Clark's remaining six children.[9] Robert likely knew when he made the request that the property could not be divided "without injury to and spoiling the whole." His request, therefore, may have been motivated by a desire to buy out his brother and sister's interests in the family businesses.

The court's reply to Robert stated: "that the said Estate could not be divided to and among the children of the said deceased John Clark, the father, without injury to and spoiling the whole." The value of the property was then determined by the court to be two thousand six hundred and forty-eight pounds, six shillings and eightpence. After the valuation was determined, Robert Clark asked the court to give him the property in exchange for compensating his brother and sisters for their shares. The court agreed and established that Robert should pay each of his siblings seven hundred and fifty-four pounds, two shillings and five pence in exchange for the ownership of the property and businesses. Robert was to pay his brother, and four sisters the money owed them by April 19, 1803 or the agreement would be invalid.[10]

Having made an installment on Flam's Landing the previous year as well as his father's property and businesses on the Cumberland County side of the river, a question arises as to where Robert secured the funding to make these purchases? Although Flam's and his father's properties were both paid for over time, both required down payments. No information has been uncovered to answer this question, but it is likely Robert earned at least some of his money from his profession as a surveyor. The earliest account of Robert being a surveyor can be found in the Septennial Census, 1800 Returns (See Figure 9).[11] When the 1850 U.S. Census was taken, Robert was listed as being 70 years old. This would mean when

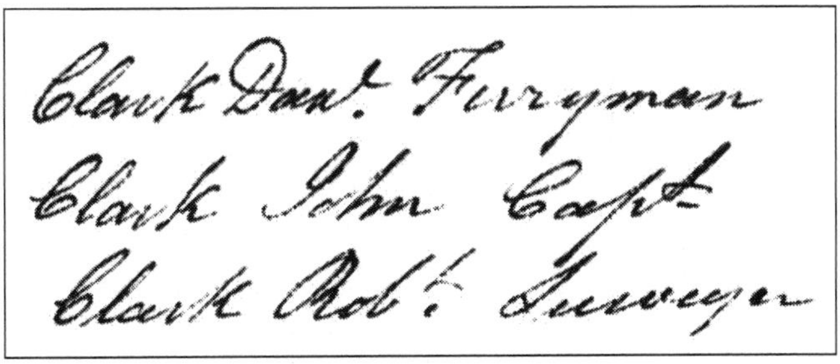

FIGURE 9: 1800 SEPTENNIAL CENSUS RETURNS, RYE TOWNSHIP, CUMBERLAND COUNTY, PENNSYLVANIA

the 1800 Septennial Census was taken, he would have been a youthful twenty years of age. [12]

By 1804, when Robert took ownership of Mathias Flam's Landing and Clark's Tavern, Ferry, and farm, an increasing number of settlers were moving westward on newly constructed turnpikes.[13] Some turnpikes carried so much traffic that during bad weather, ferry crossings like the Clark's became bottlenecks. Travelers often had to wait for days to cross on a ferry.[14] It evidently became obvious to Robert that the size of his tavern would no longer meet the needs of his growing numbers of customers.

In 1804, Clark's Tavern still consisted of its original two stages. The first stage was the Goudys' log house. Added onto it, was the second stage, the first stone addition. With ever-increasing traffic crossing the Susquehanna River on Clark's Ferry, A third stage (a second stone addition) was probably built by Robert Clark sometime between 1805 and 1808. Before 1805, Robert Clark's finances were likely tied up in buying in installments Flam's Ferry Landing on the eastern side of the Susquehanna River and Clarks' Tavern, Ferry, and farm on the western side.[15] It is likely the third stage/second stone addition was finished by 1808. That year, Robert invested in and became part-owner of the Juniata Stage Company.

The third stage/second stone addition was added to the back of the tavern giving it an "L" shape. The addition was larger than the earlier log cabin and stone section combined. As such, it likely freed up the original log and stone parts for the Clark family's private use. Up until the completion of the second addition, both tavern patrons and Clark family members would have had to share the same facilities. This would have been, at times, not only very crowded, but chaotic. Taken in 1800, the Federal Census shows nine Clark family members living in the tavern. By the time of the 1810 U.S. Census was taken, the second stone addition would have been constructed and living conditions improved for the Clark family. The 1810 Census shows four adult white males, three adult females, and one slave living at the tavern.[16] The conditions for the family were still crowded, but at least they would have likely had their own private living area in one of the sections of the tavern.

A more detailed description of the sections of the tavern building can be found in Part 2 of this book, "A Preliminary Study of the Architectural Features of Clark's Tavern, Duncannon, PA."

A Man of the Outdoors

Although listed as a surveyor in the Septennial Census of 1800, the earliest example uncovered of Robert Clark's survey work is a map completed by him in 1804. On June 6th of that year, Robert gave a survey map he had drawn to Justice of the Peace, Pat Mc Naughton. The map was a survey of a road from Brightfield's Run near McGinnes' Sawmill to (Mary) Clark's Ferry on the Susquehanna River (See Appendix, Map 1).[17] Mary Clark's Ferry was up the Susquehanna river from the location of today's Clark's Ferry Bridge. No familial connection has been found between Mary Clark and the Clark family of Clark's Tavern.

Although Robert assuredly continued surveying during the following years, the next map of his to be found was from eight years later. On March 11, 1812, Robert completed a survey map of a road that began at the Great Road that led from Harrisburg to Huntingdon and intersected the Great Road from Clark's Ferry to Sherman's Valley (See Appendix, Map 2).[18]

On April 5 of 1814 and again in 1815, two years after the Great Road Map, Robert was appointed Deputy Surveyor for Cumberland County.

In the following two years, Robert worked on a two-part project. The first part of the project was a Draft of a Road from Sheep Island in Rye Township to Clark's Ferry (See Appendix, Map 3.) He completed the map on December 27, 1815. This was more-or-less a rough draft.[19] The following year, on May 28, 1816, he completed a more finished survey map of the road (See Appendix, Map 4).[20]

Two years after his Sheep Island to Clark's Ferry map, on October 14, 1818, Robert completed a survey map of the road from Thomas Huling's Ferry on the Juniata River to the Public Road Leading Up the Juniata River (See Appendix, Map 5).[21]

Robert continued surveying in 1819. On March 26th and 27th of that year, he completed a survey draft of a road from Clark's Ferry to a point on the Juniata River across from Sheep Island (See Appendix, Map 6).[22] This road eventually became the part of North Market Street in Duncannon that went from Clark's Tavern to the Newport Road (Route 849). It then continued up the Juniata River to a point across from Sheep Island.

Five years later, on April 13, 1824, Robert gave to Cumberland County Court, a description (viewing) of a proposed road from the Great Northern Turnpike Road, near the mouth of the Juniata River, to near New Berry's Falls (See Appendix, Map 7).[23]

Later that year, on December 23, 1824, Robert Clark's survey skills were used by the Pennsylvania State Legislature. On that date, Robert, along with John Cox from Franklin County and John Harper from Cumberland County, were authorized by the state to survey the legal boundary line between Cumberland and Perry Counties[24] Perry County had been created from the northern part of Cumberland County in 1820. Perhaps, since this was the last of Robert Clark's survey assignments to be uncovered, he may have retired his surveyor's compass (circumferentor), and Gunter chain after this assignment to allow more time for his many other enterprises.

NEW TRANSPORTATION ENTERPRISES

In 1806, the first petitions were submitted to the state government to construct a turnpike from Harrisburg to Pittsburgh. It was to go up the Susquehanna River from Harrisburg to Robert Clark's Ferry Landing in Dauphin County. After crossing on Clark's Ferry to Cumberland County, it would go up the Juniata River, eventually ending in Pittsburgh. Responding to the petition, on March 4, 1807, the Commonwealth passed an act incorporating a company to build the road. Shortly after the turnpike company was created, the Juniata Mail Stage Company was formed to run a stagecoach line from Harrisburg to Alexandria, Pennsylvania.[25]

Robert invested in the new stagecoach company in 1808. He partnered with six other men to start the Juniata Mail Stage. The new stagecoach line started in Harrisburg on May 3, 1808. Its regular route started at Harrisburg on a Wednesday morning. It would then travel by way of Clark's Ferry to Millerstown, Thompson, Mifflintown, Lewistown,

Waynesburg, and Huntingdon arriving at Alexandria on Friday. The coach would then return to Harrisburg by the same route. They arrived back at Harrisburg the next Tuesday morning.

The company advertised "elegant and convenient Carriages, good Horses, and careful drivers." In their advertisement, they went on to say that their passengers would be "rendered safe, easy and agreeable."

The fair for such luxurious transportation was six cents a mile. Each passenger could take with them fourteen pounds of baggage without being charged. The advertisement ended with "Horses and chairs will be procured at the different towns, for those passengers who wish to go off the road or proceed further than Alexandria."[26] "From 1808 to the time of the packet-boats, about 1836, Clark's Tavern was a place of daily resort for people of the vicinity when the stages halted at the old hostelry."[27]

The stage company financially benefited Robert Clark in several ways. Besides money earned by being a partner in the company, Robert made money when the stage crossed on Clark's Ferry two times a week. In addition, many of the stage's passengers would have bought food and drink at Clark's Tavern and perhaps lodged overnight.

Until 1808, most patrons lodging at Clark's Tavern would have been traveling men. They would have slept in communal bedrooms, sometimes two or three to a bed, and would have eaten communally in the tavern's public or bar room. With wealthier clientele (now including women) arriving on stagecoaches, many of these passengers would have expected private facilities and better services. It is likely because of these expectations; the tavern's second stone addition had been completed by c. 1808. The new addition would have provided both private bedrooms and a private dining room for those who could afford them. As a result, hard cider, ale, and whiskey were probably not enough to satisfy the palates of these new upper-class patrons. In 1809, Robert wrote a letter to John Foster in Harrisburg ordering "wine and spirits."[28]

Twelve years later, evidently encouraged by the success of the Juniata Mail Stage, on July 12, 1820, Robert advertised in the *Perry Forester,* a new stagecoach company he was starting. The new company was the Harrisburg and Bellefonte Mail Stage. The stage started its first run on April 1, 1821. On the 1st, it left Buffington's Inn in Harrisburg at noon.

By way of Clark's Tavern it arrived at Bellefonte Sunday afternoon. It then left Bellefonte for Harrisburg on Wednesday morning and arrive back at Harrisburg Friday morning. The following were the fares:

From Harrisburg to Clark's Ferry $1.00
From Clark's Ferry to Millerstown $1.00
From Millerstown to Lewistown $2.00
From Lewistown to Bellefonte $2.00
From Harrisburg to Bellefonte $6.00

"Way passengers" (passengers going just partway between stops) would be charged seven cents a mile. Each passenger would be allowed seventeen pounds of baggage. All baggage above seventeen pounds would be charged "at the rate of proportion." In his advertisement, Robert made the disclaimer that all baggage was carried by the stagecoach at the passenger's own risk.[29]

Robert must have contracted "stagecoach fever" as one year after he began his Harrisburg and Bellefonte Stage Line, on April 11, 1822, he announced the start of his second stage line. In the *Perry Forester,* he announced his new mail stagecoach route would run between Clark's Ferry and Concord in Franklin County. In the advertisement, he stated that the coach left Clark's Ferry "every Wednesday morning at 4 o'clock." It then stopped at Landisburg, where passengers could have breakfast. After breakfast, the coach left and arrived at Concord that evening. The stagecoach then left for Clark's Ferry the next morning and arrived back at Clark's Ferry that evening. From Clark 's Ferry to Landisburg, the fare was $1.00. From Landisburg to Concord, it was $1.25. Passengers riding partway were charged six cents per quarter-mile. Each passenger on the stage could take fourteen pounds of baggage. Any baggage above that weight would be charged "150 pounds at the weight of a passenger, great or less weight in proportion." Robert finished his advertisement with his usual disclaimer that "All baggage at the risk of the owner."[30]

On October 23, 1822, Robert announced an expansion of his Belle-fonte Stage Line. The new route continued from Bellefonte to Meadville, making stops along the way at Philipsburg and Franklin.[31]

Stage fare reduced on the Northern Route turnpike road from Harrisburg to Pittsburg.

THE Stage proprietors on the above route have determined on running their Stages three times a week, to run through in less than four days, leave Harrisburg and Pittsburg respectively every Tuesday, Thursday and Saturday mornings.

Fare for the whole distance $10 00
Way Passengers six cents per mile
All Baggage at the risk of the owners.

By the above arrangement passengers going to or from Baltimore or to or from Philadelphia either by the Lancaster or Reading route will be certain of passing on without delay or disappointment. In addition to a connexion with the Baltimore and Philadelphia line of Stages at Harrisburg our line will connect at Pittsburg with the Washington, Beaver and Erie Stages, which will accommodate travellers to any part of the western country. The Bellefonte and Erie stage leaves Harrisburg every Tuesday and Saturday mornings.

John Blair & Co.
&
Robert Clark.

. The Printers who have formerly inserted advertisements for this line of Stages will be so good as to insert this.

FIGURE 10: STAGE FARE REDUCED
Front page classified advertisement, *Oracle of Dauphin*, Harrisburg,
April 23, 1825, Vol. xxiv, No 30

Three years later, on March 23, 1825, Robert Clark began another stagecoach line, the Clark's Ferry to Blain. This time, he advertised a stage that started at Clark's Ferry and went through New Bloomfield and Ickesburg to Landisburg in one day. The following day, the stage went to Blain by way of Landisburg. On the third day, the stage went back by way of Landisburg to Ickesburg. On the fourth day, the stage returned to Clark's Ferry by way of Bloomfield.[32]

By April 23, 1825, the Juniata Mail Stage had extended its route from Harrisburg to Pittsburg on the Northern Route Turnpike. On Saturday, April 25th, Robert Clark and his partners posted an advertisement in Harrisburg's *Oracle of Dauphin* (See Figure 10).

In the advertisement, they stated they had reduced their fares. The cost of the total trip from Harrisburg to Pittsburgh would now be $10.00. Passengers riding only part of the way would be charged six cents a mile, and, of course, baggage was "at the risk of the owners." Their stagecoaches would run three times a week, leaving each Tuesday, Thursday, and Saturday morning. The total trip from Harrisburg to Pittsburgh would take "less than four days."[33]

Robert continued having stagecoach fever. He began his last stagecoach route on June 12, 1828, the Millerstown to Carlisle Stage Line. This stagecoach left Millerstown on Thursday morning at 6 o'clock. It went by way of Milford and Bloomfield to Landisburg. The stage then returned to Millerstown in the afternoon by the same route. The coach then left from Millerstown at 6 o'clock on Friday morning. It went by way of Liverpool, Montgomery's Ferry, Thompson's Crossroads, and Clark's Ferry to Bloomfield. The following morning, Saturday, the stage left Bloomfield and went to Carlisle by way of Landisburg and Sterrett's Gap. Although its return route was not uncovered, it likely followed the same route back to Millerstown.[34]

No primary information on how long Robert Clark's stage lines lasted was uncovered. H. H. Hain, in his *History of Perry County*, states that "Clark abandoned the lines after a time and the mails were again carried by post riders until the advent of the Rice Stage Line."[35]

ROBERT CLARK'S OTHER CUMBERLAND COUNTY BUSINESSES

Most people's time and energy would have been totally consumed surveying, running a tavern, ferry, and farm, but not Robert Clark. Around 1810, he joined in a partnership with William Ramsey and John Boden to build a stone gristmill on the Little Juniata Creek. By that time,

Ramsey had become a lawyer in Carlisle and Robert's brother-in-law, while Boden was a cashier in a Carlisle Bank. The next year, John would also become Robert's brother-in-law.[36] To build the mill, the trio hired the previously mentioned John Chisholm, from Inverness, Scotland. The building of the mill began in 1814 and went into operation on July 4, 1817. It was run for many years by Chisholm and sold by Robert, John, and William about 1839.[37]

By 1814, when the construction of the grist mill began, Robert Clark had extensively expanded his investments in Cumberland County. That year, besides John Clark's original 215 acres, he was taxed in Rye Township for three additional tracts of land; one tract of 150 acres and the other two for 50 and 53 acres. This totaled 468 acres in all. In addition, he was taxed for 1 gristmill, 2 sawmills, 1 ferry, 2 lots in Petersburg, 3 horses, and 3 cows. The gristmill was privately owned by him and was not the one being built at that time by John Chisholm.[38]

During the following three years, Robert continued to accumulate his land holdings in Rye Township, Cumberland County. In his 1817 taxes, he was taxed for a total of 580 acres. These were described as 210 patented acres, 250 warranted acres, 70 patented acres on the north side of Sherman's Creek, and 50 patented acres on the south side of the creek. The acreage on the north and south sides of the creek were the locations for his Sherman's Creek Ferry Landings. This was the first year he was taxed for his Sherman's Creek Ferry. The same year he was also taxed for a grist and saw-mill and his ferry on the Susquehanna River.[39]

By 1820, when Perry County was created out of Cumberland County, Robert had increased his land holdings in Rye Township, Perry County, to 655 acres. This was 75 more acres than he was taxed for in 1817. He was still taxed that year for a ferry on the Susquehanna River and for one on Sherman's Creek. In addition, with his partners Boden and Ramsey, he was taxed for 266 acres and a grist and sawmill. He also owned five lots, two with houses, in the nearby village of Petersburg.[40] The village was downriver, about one-half mile, from Clark's Tavern and Landing. Christian Miller had laid out the village with lots to sell in September of 1792. Over time, the village became the nucleus for the current Borough of Duncannon.[41]

A GREAT OPPORTUNITY GONE BUST

On May 8, 1818, John Boden, Robert Clark's brother-in-law, placed an advertisement in the *Carlisle Gazette*. It stated that in an act passed by the Pennsylvania State Legislature, the state had decided to erect "a permanent (canal) bridge over the river Susquehanna at or near Clark's Ferry in the counties of Dauphin and Cumberland." The purpose of Boden's advertisement was to notify the men of both Dauphin and Cumberland Counties that there was going to be a meeting of a bridge committee at Clark's Tavern on Wednesday, June 3rd. Robert Clark was one of the committee members, and John Boden was its chairman.[42] The committee likely wanted to investigate possible economic opportunities presented by building the canal bridge at Clark's Ferry. The state legislature, however, did not pass legislation to begin the project until 1824. Robert no doubt saw this as a money-making opportunity for him in both Cumberland and Dauphin Counties.

As has been discussed, Robert first began investing in Dauphin County in 1800. In 1801, he began buying in installments the 50-acre tract known as Huling's/Flam's Landing. In 1804, Robert paid off his debt to Mathias Flam and took total ownership of his landing, property, and improvements.

During the next 20 years, Robert kept these 50 acres while buying and selling in Dauphin County an additional 172½ acres. By 1824, he was back to owning just his original 50 acres plus 1 island in the Susquehanna River.[43] It is important to note that in 1824, he was also taxed for the first time for two ferries (ferry landings). These became known as Clark's Upper and Lower Ferries.[44]

The exact date when Robert began his Upper Ferry has not been uncovered. The 1822 Turnpike Map from Harrisburg to Millerstown shows Clark's Lower Ferry Landing along the proposed turnpike (See Figure 11). The surname of the person leasing Robert's tavern building at that time was Jones.[45]

Although the turnpike is shown going to the location of Clark's Upper Ferry and later Clark's Ferry Bridge, no ferry crossing is shown. It is

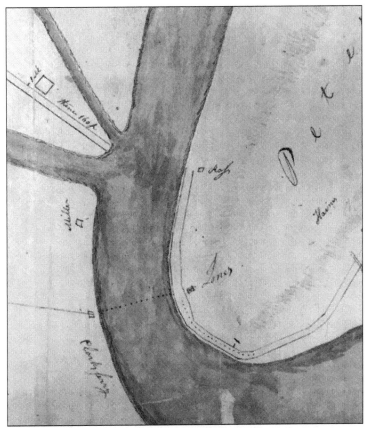

FIGURE II: PART OF DRAUGHT OF TURNPIKE FROM HARRISBURG TO
MILLERSTOWN, JUNE 1822

likely Robert Clark established his Upper Ferry sometime between 1822
when the turnpike draft was drawn and 1824 when Halifax Township's
taxes listed him as having two ferries.

Robert began investing heavily in Halifax Township, Dauphin
County, after 1824. By 1827, he was taxed in Halifax Township, Dauphin County for 300 acres of land, two stone houses (tavern buildings),
and 2 ferries.[46] By 1836 when he sold his last Dauphin County property,
he had owned, at one time or another, eight properties totaling 503 acres
as well as three islands in the Susquehanna River (See Figure 12).

A general description of the properties Robert Clark owned in Dauphin County in 1830 can be found in a report he gave to the Board

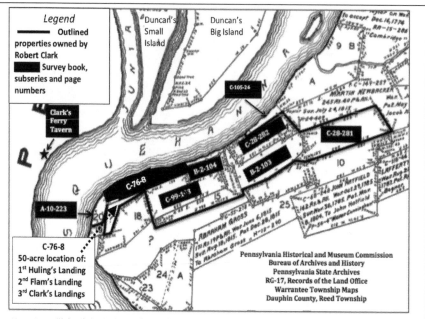

Note: 3 small islands in the Susquehanna River east of Duncan's Big Island (today Haldeman's) were also warranted to Robert Clark. Their survey books, subseries and pages are A-23-1, A-23-2 and A-10-224.

Robert Clark's East Shore Properties Across from Clark's Tavern

Survey Book, Subseries & Page	Grantee	Date Surveyed For Robert Clark	Acreage	Original Warrantee	Warrant Date
B-2- 103	Robert Clark	5 April 1813	89 ac. 140p	Mathias Flam	6 March 1794
C-28-281	Robert Clark	20 July 1815	108 ac.	Robert Clark	20 June 1814
C-28-282	Robert Clark	30 & 31 Oct. 1818	54 ac. 80p.	Robert Clark	20 June 1814
B-2-104	Robert Clark	5 October 1819	79 ac. 80 p	William Power	27 March 1788
A-10-223	Robert Clark	10 October 1819	10 ac. 90 p.	Robert Clark	20 June 1814
C-105-24	Robert Clark	22 June 1832	11 ac.	Abraham Jones	27 April 1767
C-99-163	Robert Clark	9 May 1833	100 ac.	Marcus Huling	17 December 1774
C-76-8	Robert Clark	c. 1801-1804	50	Marcus Huling	1 June 1767
		TOTAL	503 ac. 70 p.		

FIGURE 12: COMPOSITE WARRANTEE MAP BY AUTHOR SHOWING PROPERTIES OWNED IN DAUPHIN COUNTY BY ROBERT CLARK

of Canal Commissioners on March 15th of that year. In the report, he stated that he owned around three hundred acres of land that ran for about a mile along the Susquehanna River banks. This was the amount of acreage previously mentioned in Robert Clark's 1827 Halifax Township, Dauphin County Taxes. He went on to state that the tract of land was mostly a mountain ledge, producing some timber, but not fit for farming. Robert then stated that a public road ran through his property along the bank of the river. Along the bank, the road connected three of his ferry landings. Two of the landings had houses that were used as taverns. Associated with the taverns were stables and other outbuildings.[47]

It was not likely just a coincidence that Robert began investing in Dauphin County property after 1824. On March 27th of that year, the Pennsylvania State Legislature passed the first of three Pennsylvania Canal Acts. The first act empowered then-Governor John A. Shulze to appoint three commissioners to find the best locations for a Pennsylvania Canal.[48]

On April 11th of the following year, 1825, a second act was passed that appointed two more canal commissioners. The five commissioners were empowered to hire surveyors and other personnel to "aid them in examining several waterways and proposed canal routes." A decision was made to survey possible routes up the east bank of the Susquehanna in Dauphin County. It was to be built from Swatara Creek past Harrisburg to the vicinity of Clark's Ferry. This branch of the Pennsylvania Canal was labeled the Eastern Division.[49] Another branch of the canal to be surveyed was the Susquehanna Division. It was to be constructed down the eastern side of the Susquehanna River from a point across from Northumberland. It was to meet with the Eastern Division in Dauphin County at or near Clark's Ferry.

The Juniata was the third Division of the canal. The first leg of the canal was to come down the Juniata River from Lewistown and terminate just below the junction of the Juniata and Susquehanna Rivers. It was to terminate in the vicinity of Clark's Ferry's Perry County landing. The Juniata Division, on the west bank of the Susquehanna, would then be joined by a canal bridge with the Susquehanna and Eastern Divisions on the east side of the river.[50]

On February 25, 1826, a third act of the Pennsylvania State Legislature was enacted. It allowed the canal commissioners to start constructing the canals.[51] The location where the three canals joined would economically either make-or-break Robert Clark.

Until the following year, 1827, Robert's economic prospects in Dauphin County looked good. In 1827, he owned 300 acres, two wooden houses, three stone buildings (two of which he leased as taverns), and two ferry landings, an Upper and a Lower. The taverns and landings were on opposite ends of the fifty acres he had bought from Mathias Flam in 1804.

The ferry landing used by Robert Clark for his Lower Ferry was originally Flam's Landing. It had been used by John and Daniel Clark when they started their ferry in 1788. The Landing was located above Foster's Falls at the southern end of the fifty-acre tract (See Figure 13).

Robert's Upper Ferry Landing was in the vicinity of Huling's and later Ellis' former ferry landing. It was located at the northern end of the fifty-acre tract across from Duncan's Island. It was in the vicinity of where Clark's Ferry Bridge is today. Clark's Ferry Bridge was thus named after Clark's Upper Ferry and not, as usually thought, his Lower Ferry.[52]

In building the canal along the Susquehanna River, two problems presented themselves to the state. The first was how to transport the canal boats across the river. One possible solution was to carry the boats across on an "aqueduct" or water bridge. A second possible type of bridge that could be used to pull the boats across the river was a towpath bridge. With this type a bridge, a dam was usually built across a body of water below the bridge. The dam would create a pool upon which canal boats could be floated. From the bridge, draft animals would then pull the boats across the pool of water.[53]

A second and related problem for the state was where to build the bridge across the Susquehanna. Two possible solutions presented themselves.

One possible location was between Clark's Lower Ferry Landing and Foster's Falls (See Figure 13). Foster's Falls are rapids running across the Susquehanna River at the end of Peter's Mountain.

Another possible location for the canal bridge was at Clark's Upper Ferry Landing. At this location, the eastern terminus of the bridge would be Clark's Landing and the western terminus, the southern end of Duncan's Island (See Figure 13).

Because of the potential economic opportunities envisioned by Robert Clark and the people of Perry County, they hoped the bridge would be built at Clark's Lower Ferry. This sentiment would be taken into consideration by the Pennsylvania Canal Commission when determining the location of the bridge, but in the end, costs would determine where the bridge would be built.

On February 5, 1827, after a vote of approval by the Canal Commissioners, Governor John A. Shulze approved an extension and alteration of the Eastern Division of the canal from Harrisburg up to Foster's

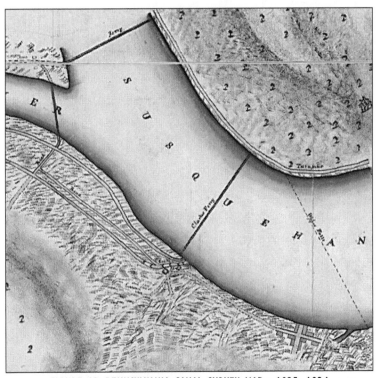

FIGURE 13: PENNSYLVANIA CANAL SURVEY MAP, c.1825–1826
Shows possible canal routes to Clark's Lower Ferry

Falls, just below Clark's Lower Ferry Landing.[54] By February 5th of that year, the question as to where to cross the Susquehanna had not yet been decided. Building the canal bridge between Clark's Lower Ferry Landing and Foster's Falls would leave Robert Clark's Lower Ferry still in operation and provide other business opportunities for him and the people of Perry County. Building the canal bridge at Robert's Upper Ferry Landing, on the other hand, would severely damage his investments in both Perry and Dauphin Counties and bypass Perry County. In building the canal to Clark's Upper Ferry Landing, contractors would construct the canal along the edge of the river through Robert's fifty-acre tract. As they excavated the canal, they would destroy everything in their path. This included Clark's Lower Ferry Landing and many of Robert's improvements. The contractors would also use many of Robert Clark's natural resources.

Six months after approving the extension of the canal, on August 2, 1827, engineers gave the Canal commissioners cost estimates for building an aqueduct and a towpath bridge at both Clark's Upper and Clark's Lower Ferry Landings (See Figure14).[55]

Analysis of the chart shows that the engineers predicted it would cost the state less to cross the Susquehanna River using a towpath bridge at Clark's Upper Ferry Landing. The additional costs incurred crossing at Clark's Lower Ferry were estimated to be considerably more because of the additional span of the river. The span of the river at Clark's Lower Ferry was "more than eight hundred feet" longer than at the Upper Landing.[56]

At the meeting on August 2, 1827, the Canal Board, decided to build a combination tow-path-turnpike bridge from Clark's Upper Ferry

---

FIGURE 14: PROJECTED COSTS OF BRIDGING THE SUSQUEHANNA RIVER

Crossing by aqueduct bridge at Clark's Lower Ferry. $298,088	Crossing by high level towpath bridge at Clark's Lower Ferry. $222,666
Crossing by aqueduct bridge at Clark's Upper Ferry. $240,887	Crossing by high level towpath bridge at Clark's Upper Ferry. $152,496

Landing on the eastern shore of the Susquehanna to the tip of Duncan's Island. They stated that Clark's Upper Ferry was "the most advantageous and economical place for the crossing."[57]

On August 3rd of 1827, the Canal Board officially resolved "That the Eastern Division of the Pennsylvania canal be extended to a point at the lower end of Duncan's Island." They also decided that on August 8th, bids would be taken for construction of the dam at Duncan's Island and for construction of fourteen miles of the Eastern Division of the canal. The construction bids were to be taken at a meeting at Baskin's Tavern at Clark's Upper Ferry Landing in Dauphin County.[58]

Also, on August 3rd, formidable protests were made to the governor by "several gentlemen from Carlisle and parts of Perry County." As a result, the governor held up the canal project until after the next Canal Board meeting.[59]

On August 6th, in preparation for the August 8th meeting of contractors at Baskin's Tavern, Charles Mowry, the Acting Commissioner for the Eastern and Susquehanna Divisions of the canal, printed handbills to be passed out at the meeting. The bills announced, "Sealed proposals will be received at Baskin's Tavern, Clark's Upper Ferry, until 12 o'clock on Saturday next, the eleventh...for constructing a STONE DAM. The handbill went on to say that "the undertaker (contractor) must furnish the materials at his own expense." Since wood and stone were readily available for the taking on Robert Clark's Dauphin County land, in contrast to today's practices, materials taken would be without his permission and at Robert Clark's expense. Mowry's handbill continued, "At the same time and place, sealed proposals will be received for continuing the canal."[60] The canal was thus planned to go through and destroy Robert Clark's Lower Ferry Landing.[61]

On August 11th, the meeting to bid on the construction projects took place at Baskin's Tavern. At the meeting, Mowry later reported, "A large collection of people assembled" and "a rough sketch of a dam, profile and specifications were put up in the bar-room, and all the explanations given." 'Robert Clark was at the tavern and had a different viewpoint than most of the other men gathered there. At the gathering, he placed a piece of paper in Mowry's hand and a copy on the bar-room wall. The paper read as follows:

To C. Mowry, acting Canal Commissioner

Sir: TAKE NOTICE, That I will prosecute all and every person or persons, who shall be found on my premises, erecting any dam or dams, for the purpose of injuring any of my ferries on the Susquehanna River, or injuring any other of my property, bordering on said river.
ROBERT CLARK
Clark's Ferry, Aug. 11, 1827[62]

Later in the morning, Mowry extended his deadline for turning in proposals from 12:00 until 1:00 P.M. At 1:00 o'clock, Mowry accepted proposals for building the dam and canal. The contract for building the dam was awarded to Abbott Green and William Cameron. The dam later became known as Green's Dam. Some dispute was later created by the award as Green and Cameron were not the lowest bidders. The canal contract was awarded to Dearmond, Rodearmel, & Company.[63]

At the next Canal Board meeting held on September 10th, J. Miller of Philadelphia represented Robert Clark and the people of Perry County. Miller gave a letter and presentation to the Canal Board. In his presentation and letter, Miller first tried to convince the Board that it was financially to the state's advantage to build the bridge at Clark's Lower Ferry Landing. The presentation did not change the Board's mind as to the location of the bridge.

Mr. Miller then tried to persuade the Board to change their mind because of the economic damage that would be done to Robert Clark in building the canal to his Upper Ferry Landing. Before Miller's presentation, Robert had told him the damages to his property would amount to $20,000. When Miller gave his presentation, however, he reduced Robert's damages to $10,000. Miller added that if the Juniata Canal would be built down the west side of the river and the canal bridge cross at Clark's Lower Ferry Landing, Robert would "release all damages and offer to the state a bonus of $6,000" in either money or property. Miller finished by stating that "It is the anxious desire of at least five-sixths of the whole population of the county (Perry), that the canal should cross at Clark's (Lower) Ferry."[64]

On the same day, despite J. Miller's presentation and the hopes of Robert Clark and most of the people of Perry County, the Board of Canal Commissioners decided, "there is no just ground for departing from the decision made by resolution of August 3rd last." As such, the canal would go through Robert Clark's property to his Upper Ferry Landing. Near the landing, the Eastern and Susquehanna Divisions of the canal would be joined, and a bridge would be built across to the southern tip of Duncan's Island. The Juniata Division would be built north-and south across Duncan's Island to its southern tip. There, it would join with the combined Eastern and Susquehanna Divisions. The board stated, "that the point of Duncan's Island would be the most advantageous and economical place for crossing the river."[65] They asserted that It was economically advantageous to cross at Duncan's Island because it was "more than a thousand feet narrower" across the Susquehanna at Duncan's Island than at Clark's Lower Ferry.[66]

CONSTRUCTION AND DESTRUCTION

A year later, on December 8, 1828, C. Mowry reported that the bridge at Clark's Upper Ferry was almost completed.[67] It was a Burr-arch wooden covered bridge with an exterior towpath gallery. The gallery was designed for mules and horses to pull canal boats across the river. The interior of the covered bridge allowed pedestrians, animals, and vehicles such as wagons and stagecoaches to cross the river.[68] Mowry had predicted the bridge would be finished over the winter of 1828–1829. This was an overly optimistic projection that did not take into consideration the severe ice-floods that often occur on the Susquehanna River.

As the winter of 1828 turned into the spring of 1829, on March 26th, William Wilson, the project's engineer, authored a progress report.

The report described "the extent of the injuries occasioned by the floods and ice" to the canal projects. In the report, it stated that the bridge abutments and the dam were injured by breaking ice. The canal was undamaged, however.[69] While Robert Clark's Lower Ferry Landing was destroyed by this time, presumably, this gave Robert Clark's Upper Ferry a reprieve from becoming obsolete.

Robert Clark's grievances with canal construction through his property were formally addressed in 1830. On March 15th of that year, the president of the Board of Canal Commissioners, Mr. Scott, laid before the Canal Board a petition and documents from Robert Clark. The papers were a request from Robert Clark for compensation "for damages to his property at Clark's Ferry" as a result of building the canal, dam, and bridge.[70] Robert's petition and papers were not taken up until four days later on March 19th. On that date, they were read to the Board. One part of the papers described the amount of property he owned in Dauphin County, and another part gave Robert's claims for damages from building the canal, dam, and bridge. His claims for damages follow:

Destruction of wood $350
Stone taken 12,500
Destruction of stables. .500
Injuries done his ferries and consequent
    uselessness of his ferry craft 30,300
_____
Total . . . . **$43,650**[71]

The Board's responses to Robert's claims for damages certainly disappointed him. For the destruction of his timber, the Board concluded that since the wood was taken by contractors and laborers for their own use and without asking permission from the Commonwealth, the state was not responsible. For stone taken, the Board stated that since Robert's "stone quarries be inexhaustible," and it would cost too much to bring in the stone, nothing would be paid to Robert for his stone. For the destruction of Robert's stables and "other injuries, done to his improvements," the Board recommended Robert be compensated $500. They believed this was "a liberal compensation" for the destruction. And finally, Robert must have been most disappointed by the lack of compensation for the loss of his ferry business. For the loss of his ferry business, the Canal Board stated that since "the damages which he will sustain will be merely consequential . . . the Board cannot under any existing law, compensate him for the injury". As a result, the Committee resolved that "the Eastern Division of the Penna. Canal, be authorized to pay Robert Clark, five hundred dollars in full for damages sustained in the construction of the public works through his property, at Peter's Mountain."[72]

Robert Clark's request for compensation was once again considered at the next Canal Board meeting on September 25, 1830. At the meeting, Robert made a presentation to the Committee in which he stated that the Superintendent of the Eastern Division had offered him $1,000 in compensation. The Board determined this was fair, "but a Mr. Mitchel stated that since the sum of the reimbursement was supposed to take into consideration losses from his ferry businesses, the amount was too small." A final decision on the amount of Robert's compensation was not made.[73]

On a follow-up meeting of the Canal Board on November 29, 1830, a final motion in regards to Robert Clark's compensation was laid before the Board. The motion was accepted to award Robert Clark $2,100. One month later, on December 31, 1830, Robert Clark was paid $2,100 in compensation for his losses.[74]

As for the status of Clark's Ferry Bridge, by 1830, the water and ice of the winter of 1829–1830 and defects in the bridge made it unsafe. Repairs were not completed, and the bridge made safe until November 15, 1832. On that date, the Superintendent of the Eastern Division of the Canal reported that "Clark's Ferry bridge has undergone a thorough repair, the original defects in that structure have been remedied" and the bridge was declared safe to use.[75]

During the next four winters, however, damage from water and ice continued to take its toll on both the bridge and dam, closing down the bridge and making the canal periodically useless. So many bridge problems occurred that, on March 16, 1836, the Pennsylvania Senate and House of Representatives voted to require the Canal commissioners

FIGURE 15: EARLIEST KNOWN DEPICTION OF CLARK'S FERRY AND BRIDGE
Watercolor by August Killner (Courtesy of the Pennsylvania State Library, Harrisburg, Pennsylvania)

to build a new bridge at the same location over the Susquehanna "during the coming season." The new bridge was to start being built on January 26, 1837.[76] Ice flooding continued to vex the engineers building the bridge.[77] As a result, the new bridge was "passable" by March 1838, but still not entirely completed on December 21, 1838. The earliest depiction of Clark's Ferry Bridge by August Killner was of the second bridge (See Figure 15). To date, there have been seven bridges built at the location of Clark's Upper Ferry Crossing.[78]

In 1831, while the Commonwealth was still trying to make Clark's Ferry Bridge safe, Robert Clark likely continued to run his Upper Ferry. In Halifax Township, his taxes show he was still leasing both his Upper and Lower Ferry tavern buildings. The Upper Tavern building at the bridge was leased and run by Cornelius Baskin. The valuation of the yearly rental for his tavern was $150. The valuation of the rental at Clark's Lower Tavern leased by Jacob Fester was also $150.[79]

By 1832, Robert evidently saw a way to make a profit on three of his Dauphin County tracts of land. On June 29th of that year, he sold three tracts of his land to Harrisburg businessmen Jacob Haldeman and Thomas Elder for $1,000. The tracts were above and east of Clark's Upper Ferry Landing.[80] He continued to keep the 50-acre tract of land on which his Lower and Upper Ferry Taverns were located.

The following year, 1833, both of Robert's tavern buildings were still in operation. Cornelius Baskin rented and ran the Upper Tavern for $120 a year until June of that year. At that time, Robert started leasing the tavern to Sterrett Ramsey of Carlisle who, in-turn, advertised the tavern to sublease.[81] In 1833, Jacob Fester still rented and ran the Lower Tavern for a rent of $150 a year.[82]

In 1834, Robert continued leasing his Upper and Lower Ferry Taverns. John Martin leased the Lower Ferry Tavern for $150 for the year while the Upper Ferry Tavern was leased to James Freeland for $225. Robert's Upper Ferry Tavern business seemed to have picked up, perhaps from bridge traffic after the bridge was open.[83]

In 1835, John Martin's lease for the Lower Tavern was still $150, but for unknown reasons, James Freeland's lease for the Upper Tavern had been reduced to $175. Problems with the canal bridge or weather may have affected the business of the Upper Tavern.[84]

In 1836, the same year, the state legislature decided that the first Clark's Ferry Bridge was inadequate, and to replace it with a new bridge, Robert Clark decided to sell his remaining three tracts of land in Dauphin County. His marriage to Margaretta Bovard the year before may have had something to do with this decision. In 1836, Robert and his new wife sold their last three tracts of land in Halifax Township and their three islands in the Susquehanna River. They sold their properties to Jacob Haldeman for $1,200. One of these tracts was the 50-acres on which Clarks' Lower and Upper Tavern buildings were located along with the Upper Ferry Landing. Along with their property, the Clarks sold their ferry rights on the Susquehanna River to Haldeman.[85] The following year, 1837, Halifax Township's taxes show Haldeman's Tavern Stand at Clark's Ferry Bridge run by Benjamin Richards. The "Old Ferry

House"at Clark's former Lower Ferry Landing was run by the Widow Freeland.[86]

Although no records have been uncovered that gives an exact year when crossing the Susquehanna River on Clark's Upper Ferry came to and, it is likely to have been between 1828 and 1831. On Robert Clark's 1828 Halifax Township taxes, he is taxed for two ferries. When the next taxes were taken in 1831, no ferries were shown being taxed.[87] For certain, Robert would have had no ferry services after August 1, 1836, when he and his wife, Margaretta, sold their last Dauphin County properties and their ferry rights to Jacob Haldeman.[88]

ROBERT CLARK'S PERSONAL LIFE

Besides the deaths of his father and two elder brothers, the earliest memorable personal experience recorded in Robert Clark's life took place on June 15, 1804. On that date, one of his sisters, Nancy (Ann), was married to William Ramsey at Clark's Tavern. Nancy/Ann Clark was one of the Clark family's youngest siblings and was the first Clark to be married at the tavern. She was married to William Ramsey by Presbyterian Minister, the Reverend John Linn. Since Ramsey was the deputy-surveyor for Cumberland County at the time of his marriage, Robert likely knew him through surveying.[89] Robert owned the tavern and family businesses by the time of the marriage, and with the previous deaths of his father and two elder brothers, he was the family patriarch.

The next record of Robert's personal experiences came seven years later in 1811. In April of that year, Robert became involved in local government when he was appointed Deputy Constable of Rye Township, Cumberland County.[90] On the 28th of the following November, Jane, another one of Robert's younger sisters, married John Boden at Clark's Tavern. At the time of their wedding, John Boden was the High Sheriff of Cumberland County. Jane and John were married at Clark's Tavern by Presbyterian Minister, the Reverend Mr. Brady.[91] When the War of 1812 commenced the next year, John Boden was appointed Brigadier General for the Cumberland County Pennsylvania Militia, 1st Brigade.[92]

Probably persuaded by his brother-in-law, Brigadier General John Boden, Robert Clark joined the Pennsylvania Militia on August 7, 1814. He served for seven months as a 2nd sergeant in Company "C "under Captain J. S. Wilson. He was discharged on February 17, 1815.[93] It is not known if he participated in any military conflicts during his enlistment. While he was gone, Joseph Robison was licensed to run Clark's Tavern.[94]

No other examples of Robert's personal experiences appear until after the state legislature created Perry County from the northern part of Cumberland County on March 22, 1820.[95] On December 16th of that year, Robert Clark was reported in the *Perry Forrester* to have been appointed Justice of the Peace for Rye Township, Perry County.[96]

Two years later, on July 25, 1822, the *Perry Forester* reported that Robert had become involved with politics. The newspaper article stated that Robert was a member of the Democratic-Republican Committee.[97] The Democratic-Republican Party had been formed by Thomas Jefferson and James

FIGURE 16: VALUABLE PROPERTY FOR RENT ADVERTISEMENT
November 27, 1827, *Oracle of Dauphin*, Harrisburg, Pennsylvania

Madison from 1791–1793. It was formed to oppose the centralist policies of Alexander Hamilton and the Federalist Party. From 1801 to 1825, the party controlled Congress, the Presidency, and most state governments.[98]

On November 27, 1827, the same year the Eastern Division of the Pennsylvania Canal started construction through Robert Clark's Lower Ferry Landing in Dauphin County, Robert posted a "Valuable Property for Rent" advertisement in Harrisburg's *Oracle of Dauphin* newspaper. In the paper, he advertised a number of his properties for rent (lease). One was on the Dauphin County side of the river, and five were in what had become by that time, Perry County (See Figure 16).[99]

On the Dauphin County side of the river, Robert listed for rent (lease), his "Tavern Stand & Ferry" currently run by James Martin. It is curious Robert listed his tavern at his Lower Ferry Landing for rent since it was already rented. Perhaps with the destruction of the Lower Ferry Landing, James Martin felt leasing the tavern was no longer a good economic opportunity.

On the Perry County side of the Susquehanna, Robert advertised for rent (lease) his "WELL KNOWN TAVERN, FARM AND FERRY HOUSE, called Clark's Ferry." It is interesting to note that at the time, his brother-in-law John Boden "occupied" the tavern, i.e., ran it.

In his advertisement, he offered four other of his properties for rent in Perry County:

- A 150-acre farm (one-half cleared) that contained an operating distillery.
- A 200-acre farm in Wheatfield Township. On this property were a house, barn, gristmill, and sawmill.
- A small farm with a house and barn located at the mouth of Sherman's Creek. This was the location of Robert's Sherman's Creek Ferry.
- A farm with 500 acres of which 100 acres were "more or less" cleared. The property also contained a house and barn.

After the advertisement, no recorded personal experiences about Robert Clark's life were uncovered until 1835. That year, the trajectory of his life changed when he married Margaretta Bovard. On November 17th of that year, he was married to Margaretta by the Reverand Matthew B. Patterson at Clark's Tavern.[100] Margaretta was one of Charles Bovard's four daughters. In 1815, Charles warranted 250 acres in Saville Township and kept a tavern there until he died in 1834, the year before Margaretta and Robert were married.[101] It is likely that Robert and Margaretta's father knew each other because they were both tavern keepers. When Robert and Margaretta married, there was a considerable difference in their ages. Based on the 1850 Census, when they married, Margaretta was eighteen years of age, while Robert was fifty-five.[102] Research indicates Margaretta was Robert's first and only wife.

4

POST-FERRY TIME PERIOD
(1836–1875)

In 1836, Robert's wife Margaretta gave birth to their first child, Christina.[1] She was named after one of Robert's sisters. With his new young wife, the birth of their first child, and the slow but inevitable demise of his ferry and tavern businesses, Robert began to radically change his lifestyle. As previously discussed, he and Margaretta sold their last properties in Dauphin County the year their daughter was born.

The following year, 1837, Margaretta gave birth to their only son, John E.[2] That same year, a road was petitioned to be constructed from Petersburg to Clark's Ferry on Shearman's Creek. Robert Clark's Ferry landings were located on both sides of the creek, where it emptied into the Susquehanna River. At the creek, the petition asked for a bridge to be built. With the construction of the bridge, Clark's last ferry would be "entirely done away with."[3] An act of the Pennsylvania Legislature on April 4, 1838, resulted in the bridge being built terminating Clark's Ferry across Sherman's Creek.[4]

In 1840, Robert and his family were still living at Clark's Tavern. The U.S. Census for that year showed a male employed in agriculture at the tavern property. The male was between the ages of fifty and sixty years of age. This was likely Robert. The other male listed in the Census was under five years of age. This would have been his son, John E., who would have been three years of age at the time. In the Census, the oldest female was likely Robert's sister Christina. There were two younger females listed between the ages of twenty and thirty. One would have been Margaretta, but the name of the other female is not known. The fourth female listed was under five years of age. This would have been Robert's and Margaretta's daughter, Christina, who was four at the time. The Census was particularly interesting in that it showed one "free colored person," a female between the ages of twenty-four and thirty-six, at the tavern. Her name is not known.[5]

Two years later, Robert became seriously ill. On October 10th of 1842, he wrote his Last Will and Testament. In it, he stated, "I Robert Clark of Clark's Ferry Perry County considering the certainty of death… do make this my last will and testament."[6] In a supplement to the will written the following day, October 11th, he described two of his symptoms; "I still trust that you will see justice done to my poor children & wife or my time will be short with you - the chill has left me but still the fever." Whatever his illness, Robert, recovered and continued to live for thirteen more years.

By 1850, eight years later, the 1850 Census showed Robert, Margaretta, and their family living in Saville Township at the farm Margaretta had inherited from her father. At the time of the Census, Robert was listed as being 70 years of age, and Margaretta 33. Also living in the household, was their daughter, Christina, age 14, their son, John E., age 13 and Robert's sister, Christina, age 65.[7] There were also the following likely extended family members living with the Clarks:

- Rebecca Bovard (age 42)
- Edward Bovard (age 31)
- George Stephens (age 12)

Although Robert Clark had moved him and his family to Saville Township, he continued to own and lease the tavern. As previously discussed, both historians H.H. Hain and Francis Ellis state Robert Clark continued to lease the tavern as a house of hospitality.[8]

Five years after the 1850 Census, Robert passed away from unknown causes. He died on April 15, 1855, and was buried in Duncannon's

Presbyterian Cemetery.[9] His age at the time of his death is not clear. If he was seventy at the time of the 1850 Census, he would have been 75 in 1855. On the other hand, the notice of Robert's death in the *Perry County Democrat* was given as "about 90 years."[10] The *Freeman* reported he died at Clark's Ferry at the age of 85.[11]

Robert's will, written thirteen years earlier on October 11, 1842, was filed on May 16, 1855. The will stated:

- First that he gave his "household furniture beds and bedding no part of which shall be sold to his dearly beloved wife" to use for herself and their children and "family as it now is."
- Second, he empowered his named executors to sell the remainder of both his "Estate Real and Personal." They were to do this "at such time and upon such terms as they or the survivor of them shall deem best and after the payment of all my just debts and funeral expenses."
- Third, he bequeathed "all the rest and residue to be appropriated to the support maintenance and education of my wife my children and my Sister Christina during the minority of my said children and when my youngest child shall arrive at the age of twenty-one years then the same shall be divided equally between my wife and children or the survivor or survivors of them."

In the will, Robert went on to appoint "my dear wife Margaretta and my good friend Frederick Watts" as his executors.[12] Frederick had been his longtime neighbor and friend. He lived on the land adjacent to and north of Clark's Tavern.

It should be noted that Clark's Tavern was still owned by Robert at the time of his death but wasn't mentioned specifically in his will. Local tradition has it that after Robert Clark's death, the tavern building continued to be a place of lodging until the end of the Civil War. Local tradition also holds that on August 9, 1862, Company B of the Thirteenth Pennsylvania Reserves (part of the Pennsylvania Bucktails) mustered at the tavern.[13]

On March 17th, 18th, and 19th of 1865, the month before General Lee surrendered at Appomattox Courthouse, Clark's tavern-building and its surrounding structures were devastated by a three-day flood. Being just below the junction of the Susquehanna and Juniata Rivers, their combined forces wreaked havoc on everything in their way. Homes on North Market Street in the Borough of Duncannon were reported to be filled with five feet of water. In Duncannon, a bridge and railroad cars belonging to the Duncannon Iron Company were swept away. At Clark's Tavern building, "two barns and some other buildings" were swept away. The stone tavern building was the only structure remaining at the site when the flood ended.[14] Although still standing after the flood, the building was likely uninhabitable. In an undated newspaper article written by "the Old Timer," he described the wrecked condition of the building when he was a boy.[15] In the article, he wrote that "the south wall had fallen out and all the doors, sashes and brick had been removed." At that time, hay was being stored on the second floor at the open end of the building, and there was a hole in the roof where a chimney once stood.

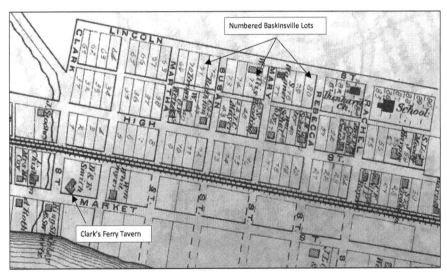

FIGURE 17: PART OF 1877 MAP OF DUNCANNON SHOWING D & E SMITH (DAVID AND ENOS) AT THE TAVERN AND BASKINSVILLE'S NUMBERED LOTS

5

POST-TAVERN TIME PERIOD
(1875–PRESENT)

The Post-tavern Time Period can be divided into four subperiods:

- Apartments, 1875–1974
- Single Dwelling/Apartments, 1974–2012
- Borough of Duncannon, 2012–2016
- Historical Society of Perry County, 2016–Present

The Post-tavern Period began in 1875 when King, Shively, and Swartz sold the ruined tavern building and four lots to two brothers, David and Enos Smith (See Figure 18).[1] By 1880, David and Enos had remodeled the tavern into four apartments. Unfortunately, they must have overextended themselves financially. On March 31, 1880, a Sheriff's Sale for the property was advertised in the newspaper, *the Perry County Democrat*. The sale advertised "a two-story stone house calculated for rental of four different families with necessary outbuildings: as the property of David and Enos Smith." The advertisement then stated that the property had been "all seized and taken in execution and to be sold by J.A. Gray, Sheriff." At the sale, on April 4,1880, two members of the same Smith family, Enos and Michael, bought back the tavern. It is not clear if Enos bought the tavern with his father named Michael, or his brother, Michael.[2]

FIGURE 18: EARLIEST KNOWN PHOTO OF CLARK'S TAVERN, c.1880
Mrs. Enos (Catherine) Smith standing in the doorway and Mrs. Katie Wetherow standing in the yard
(Courtesy of Max and Nathan Smith)

The Smith family owned and lived in the front apartment of the tavern for almost a century (See Figure 19). The front of the building had originally been remodeled into two apartments, but Enos Smith combined them into one when he and his family took up residency. The following three generations of Smiths lived in the front apartment:

- 1st – Enos and wife Catherine (Klinefelter) and their children, Minnie, Eustean, and Joseph W.
- 2nd – Joseph W. and his wife, Sarah "Catherine (Hartman) and their children, Edna, Harry, Curtis, Catherine, Max, Robert, Elsie, and Victor
- 3rd – Max and his wife, Loretta (Crouse) and their children, Cheryl, Allan, and Nathan.[3]

The other two apartments were rented, sometimes to other Smith family members, and at other times to the public.[4]

FIGURE 19: UNDATED PHOTO SHOWING THREE OF THE SMITH BROTHERS, DAVID,
JOSEPH, AND ENOS. ALSO SHOWN ARE ENOS' SON, JOSEPH W. SMITH,
PHILIP STROUSE, HARRY STROUSE, AND A. J. SEARER
(Courtesy of Max and Nathan Smith)

On August 27, 1974, Max Smith sold the tavern building to Janet
Leins and her mother, Isabel Kunkel.[5] They planned to continue renting
the apartments and eventually restore the building to its original condition.[6] The task must have been too much for Janet and her mother as five
years later, on November 10, 1979, they sold the building and its three
lots.

The building then passed through a series of owners until 2012. By
that year, it had deteriorated to the extent that it was abandoned and being
lived in by vagrants. As such, it was threatened to be demolished. To save
the historic structure, the building and two adjoining lots were bought
by the Borough of Duncannon in 2012.[7] It continued to be owned by
the Borough until 2015. Because the building needed extensive repairs
and restoration, which the Borough could not afford, on September 23,
2015, the ownership of the building was transferred to the Historical
Society of Perry County, who owns it at present.[8]

6

SUMMARY AND CONCLUSION

Crossing with the Clarks is the history of a Scottish family who settled and established successful ferry lines, a tavern, a farm, and other enterprises in the newly formed state of Pennsylvania. Their successes came from hard work, perseverance, and being at the right place at the right time. Although this book is divided into five time periods, the major focus is on the two time periods when Clark's Ferries ran across the Susquehanna River; the Early Ferry and Tavern (1787–1802) and Peak Ferry and Tavern (1802–1837).

During these two time periods, immigrants coming into Pennsylvania from Europe migrated westward. As a result, road systems were improved to meet increasing demands. With an ever-increasing number of pioneers heading west, the Clark family found an economic niche helping to fill the transportation and hospitality needs of these migrating people. Both transportation and lodging services were needed by those crossing the Susquehanna River below its junction with the Juniata River. At this location, the Scottish Clark family seized the opportunity and established successful ferry lines and a tavern.

Settling along the Susquehanna River in 1788, the Clark family had to adapt to the woodlands of Pennsylvania, having come from Scotland. Running a farm, ferry line, and rudimentary log tavern as well as raising a house full of children required a great deal of work, organization, patience, and perseverance on the part of the Clark family. By 1790, two years after starting the ferry, to accommodate every increasing patronage, the Clarks built a stone addition onto their log tavern building.

Because of the birth of a turnpike system in Pennsylvania, an ever-increasing number of people with higher economic means began to travel west by stagecoach and carriage. After crossing the Susquehanna on Clark's Ferry, this upper-class patron required and could afford better service at the tavern than was provided for the tavern's usual customers. As a result, between c. 1805 and 1808, a larger second stone addition was added to the tavern by Robert Clark. In addition to a tavern's usual pub-room and common bedrooms, this new addition had both a private dining room and private bedroom for those who could afford them.

In 1787, John Clark, the patriarch of the family, had bought the tavern property and financed Clark's Ferry. He died seven years later in 1794. Records show that from 1788 until 1799, his oldest son Daniel ran both the ferry and tavern. Perhaps because of illness, in 1799, Daniel's younger brother, Robert took over management of the Clarks' businesses. The following year, 1800, Daniel died. Robert continued running the family's businesses until 1802. That year he bought out his brother's and sisters' interests in the businesses and became the sole owner.

Having become the sole owner of Clark's Ferry, Tavern, and farm, Robert began to expand his business horizons. As an entrepreneur, he bought and sold multiple properties in both Dauphin and Cumberland/Perry Counties. In addition, In Dauphin County, he ran ferries to-and-from three ferry landings and leased two of his stone buildings as taverns. In Cumberland/Perry County, he built and owned grist and sawmills and had another ferry line crossing Sherman's Creek.

In addition to being actively involved in various businesses, Robert Clark was a surveyor and was appointed Deputy Surveyor for Cumberland County in 1814. Later that year, he enlisted for seven months in the Pennsylvania Militia during the War of 1812. After returning, in 1820, he was appointed Justice of the Peace in Rye Township and became politically active in the Democratic-Republican Committee. In 1835, at the age of fifty-five, Robert married eighteen-year-old Margaretta

Bovard. The following year, Margaretta gave birth to her and Robert's only daughter, Christina and the next year, their only son, John E.

Financially, all went well for Robert Clark until 1824. That year, the Commonwealth of Pennsylvania decided to build a canal along the Susquehanna River in Dauphin County. After traveling north past Harrisburg, the canal was designated to cross the river with a canal bridge at either Robert Clark's Upper or Lower Ferry Landing. Much to the disappointment of Robert and many of the people of Perry County, the State decided to build the canal bridge at his Upper Ferry Landing because of lower costs. When they constructed the canal along the river, north of Peter's Mountain, they dug it through Robert Clark's property. Besides destroying Clark's Lower Ferry Landing, contractors used his natural resources without his permission and destroyed two of his stables and other outbuildings. After a couple of failed attempts to receive compensation for damages done to his property and ferry business, the Commonwealth finally gave Robert $2,100 in compensation for his losses.

Robert Clark's Upper Ferry stopped running sometime between 1828 and 1831. Finally, on August 1, 1836, Robert and his wife Margaretta, sold to Jacob Haldeman the 50 acres on which the Upper Ferry Landing was located as well as their Susquehanna ferry rights. Robert Clark's Ferry business finally ended in 1837 when a bridge was built across Sherman's Creek in Perry County. Sometime after 1840, Robert and Margaretta moved with their children to a farm in Saville Township she had inherited from her father.

Robert Clark died of unknown causes on April 15, 1855, and is buried in the Duncannon Presbyterian Cemetery. After Robert's death, Margaretta married Zachariah Rice. In 1869, they sold Clark's Tavern in Duncannon and two-hundred of its acres to three investors, William King, John Shively, and Joseph Swartz. The businessmen divided the acreage into two-hundred lots to sell. When the businessmen bought the tavern, it was in a ruined condition. In 1875, the businessmen sold the uninhabitable tavern building and two adjoining lots to two brothers, David and Enos Smith. After remodeling it into apartments, in 1880, the brothers forfeited the building and lots at a sheriff's sale. At the sale,

Enos, and either his brother or father (both named Michael) regained ownership of the property. Starting with Enos, three generations of the Smith family lived in the front apartment of the building and rented the other two until Max Smith sold it in 1974.

After Max sold the property, the building went through a series of owners, gradually deteriorating to an uninhabitable condition for a second time. To save the tavern from the wrecking ball, in 2012, the Borough of Duncannon bought the tavern and its two adjoining lots. Because of a lack of funding to repair and restore the tavern, in 2015, its ownership was transferred to the Historical Society of Perry County. They are currently conducting fundraising programs to preserve and restore the building.

Although in deteriorating condition, Clark's Tavern still stands proudly today in Duncannon, Pennsylvania. It is a testament to the industriousness of three generations of the Clark family. Despite their hardships, the Clark family successfully established a farm, ferry, and tavern that contributed to the commercial and transportation history of Pennsylvania and the U.S. during the Federal and Jacksonian periods. Their enterprises were eventually made obsolete by modern progress, but their contributions are still manifested in the noble stone tavern building that was once their tavern and home.

PART II

A Preliminary Study of the Architectural Features of Clark's Tavern, Duncannon, Pennsylvania

Tavern Stages

C lark's Tavern went through three building stages. Stage 1 was Samuel Goudy's former log house. Stage 2 was John Clark's first stone addition, and Stage 3 was Robert Clark's second stone addition (See Figure 20).

Stage 1 – Goudy's Log House

In 1787, Samuel Goudy sold John Clark the property on which the Clark family built their tavern. Two houses were on the property at the time of the sale.[1]

By the following year, 1788, John and his eldest son, Daniel, had started their ferry service across the Susquehanna River. To accommodate the needs of his ferry passengers, John would have used one of Goudy's houses as an unlicensed tavern serving basic food and drink. This was Stage 1 of Clark's tavern. Although the structure no longer exists, it was probably made of log. This tradition was passed down through the Smith family, who owned the tavern building from 1880 until 1974.[2]

The earliest log part of the tavern would have been small. Based on the U.S. Direct Tax of 1798, it would have had about the same footprint as the balloon-framed structure that replaced it in the 1870s and is there

Stage 3 – Robert Clark's stone addition, c. 1805-1807

Stage 2 – John Clark's stone addition, c. 1790

Stage 1 – Samuel Goudy's log house, c. 1767

FIGURE 20: THREE STAGES OF CLARK'S TAVERN, c.1820
Based on current historical, architectural, and archaeological evidence
(Courtesy of the artist, Stephanie (Scotty Brown©)

today (See Figures 20 & 21).[3] The inside dimensions of this still standing frame structure are 11 feet by 19 feet.

It is believed that Goudy's original log structure was destroyed by a devastating three-day flood in 1865. H. H. Hain, in his *History of Perry County,* writes, "Surrounding the old stone tavern were two barns and some other outbuildings. When the water receded, the old stone tavern was found to be the only remaining structure."[4]

If the flood was powerful enough to carry away all the wooden structures on the property, it was likely to have undermined the original log part and caused it to collapse. Perhaps many, if not all, the logs were carried away. In an undated Perry County newspaper column, an author who called himself the "Old Timer" wrote, "When I was a boy, the south wall (of Clark's Tavern) had fallen out, and all the doors, sashes, and brick had been removed." The south wall was the location of the log portion of the building. He goes on to say that "Mr. Crist Klinepeter farmed for the Clarks, he stored some hay on the [open] second floor." The author then stated that there was a "hole left [in the roof] by the chimney," indicating the chimney had collapsed.[5] Although we don't know the exact date when the ruined tavern was described, it would have been between the

1865 Flood and 1875 when David and Enos Smith bought the building from King, Swartz, and Shively.[6]

STAGE 2 – FIRST STONE ADDITION
A full-Georgian two-story style house has five symmetrically placed bays or openings on each floor of the front of the house. On the first floor, the front doorway is the middle bay.

The second stage, 1st stone addition of Clark's Tavern, is a two-thirds vernacular Georgian because it only has three bays or opening on each floor instead of five. The doorway is on the left side of the building rather than in the middle. (See Figures 21 & 22). This side

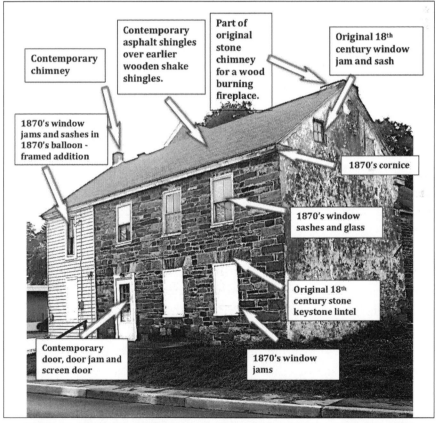

FIGURE 21: ANNOTATED PHOTOGRAPH OF FIRST STONE ADDITION (c.1790) AND LATER BALLOON-FRAME ADDITION (1870s) – NORTH MARKET STREET SIDE OF TAVERN

was originally attached to Goudy's log house (See Figure 20). In the late 1870s, a balloon-framed addition was built by David and Enos Smith on the footprint of Goudy's previously destroyed log house.[7]

Balloon-framed or light wood frame construction began in the 1830s and was used in buildings until the 1930s. It developed because of the destruction of old-growth timber in the eastern part of the United States. This type of construction used standardized two-inch lumber interior studs spaced 16 inches apart. The studs were used for vertical framing that ran from the sill to the roof. Floors were hung from the framing.[8]

The stone construction of Stage 2, the first stone addition, may have been started as early as 1789. Vertically sawn lumber was not available locally until that date.[9] The tavern was not likely completed until 1790. Daniel Clark was the first of the Clarks to be recommended by Cumberland County for a tavern license in 1790.[10]

A limited description of Stages 1 and 2 of the tavern building is found in the U.S. Direct Tax of 1798. In the tax, it describes Goudy's log house and John Clark's stone addition as one building. The description states that the building was made of wood and stone. It was two stories tall, measured 46 by 22 feet, and had twelve windows containing 144 window panes.[11]

STAGE 3 – SECOND STONE ADDITION

The third stage of the tavern, the second stone addition, was built by Robert Clark around 1805–1808. With the completion of a financially successful Philadelphia to Lancaster Turnpike in 1794, a wave of new turnpike construction began in Pennsylvania.[12] The new turnpikes brought increasing numbers of settlers and businessmen to Clark's Ferry and Tavern. These included a new class of traveler that had rarely stayed at the tavern before, those belonging to a wealthy upper-class. With improved roads, these wealthier patrons, including women, now arrived by stagecoach and carriage. Until this time, most of the travelers were working men who slept in the tavern's communal bedrooms and ate together in its public or bar room. The new upper-class patrons required a higher class of services. They wanted more privacy and better food and drink.[13]

To satisfy these wants, the Clark's needed to provide a private bedroom and a dining room. Because of a need for additional space and specialized rooms, the Clarks' second addition was larger than Stages 1 and 2 combined. Like the first addition, the second addition is made of stone. Unlike the first addition, on the Clark Street side of the building, the second addition has three bays with a doorway in the middle and a window on either side. On the Margaretta Street side, the addition has four bays on each floor with an offset doorway towards the middle of the building (See Figures 22, 31 & 32).

APARTMENT STAGE

On April 10, 1869, Margaretta Rice and her second husband, Zachariah Rice, sold the tavern and 200 of its acres to three businessmen; William King, Joseph Swartz and John Shively.[14] They subdivided the Clark

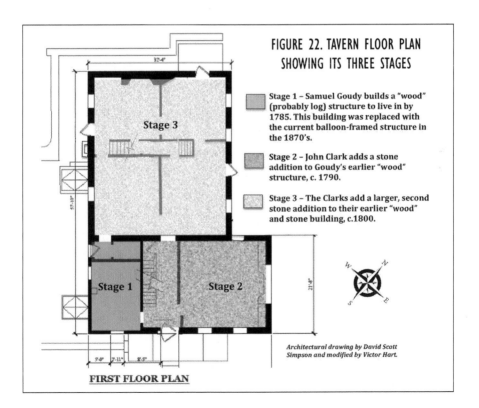

FIGURE 22. TAVERN FLOOR PLAN SHOWING ITS THREE STAGES

Stage 1 – Samuel Goudy builds a "wood" (probably log) structure to live in by 1785. This building was replaced with the current balloon-framed structure in the 1870's.

Stage 2 – John Clark adds a stone addition to Goudy's earlier "wood" structure, c. 1790.

Stage 3 – The Clarks add a larger, second stone addition to their earlier "wood" and stone building, c.1800.

Architectural drawing by David Scott Simpson and modified by Victor Hart.

FIRST FLOOR PLAN

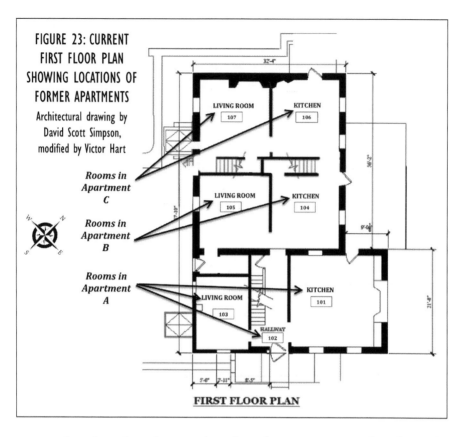

FIGURE 23: CURRENT FIRST FLOOR PLAN SHOWING LOCATIONS OF FORMER APARTMENTS

Architectural drawing by David Scott Simpson, modified by Victor Hart

Rooms in Apartment C

Rooms in Apartment B

Rooms in Apartment A

FIRST FLOOR PLAN

acreage into lots that they marketed as the community of Baskinsville (See Figure 17). In 1875, King, Swartz, and Shively sold the tavern, the lot it sits on, and two adjacent lots to brothers David and Enos Smith.[15] At that time, the two stone additions were likely in partial ruin, and Goudy's original log house was gone. In addition, the chimney on the south end of the building had collapsed, "and all the doors, sashes, and brick had been removed."[16]

As far as is known, the floor plan of the tavern building remained basically unchanged until after it was sold to the Smiths in 1875.[17] After purchasing the building, David and Enos Smiths built a balloon-framed apartment where Goudy's original log cabin had been. They joined it with the two stone additions which they had remodeled into apartments. The brothers must have had financial problems, however. The tavern and its lots were seized and sold at a sheriff sale on March 17, 1880. Before the sale, the building was advertised as being ready "for rental of four different families with necessary outbuildings." At the sale, Enos, and either his brother or father (both named Michael) bought the tavern.[18] Afterward, they converted the building into three apartments (See Figure 23). Each of the three apartments had a similar floor plan. On the first floor, each had a living room and kitchen. On the second floor, each had two bedrooms. Later, when public water and sewage became available, a back bedroom in each apartment was subdivided into a bath, a small hallway, and a small bedroom. For this discussion, the three apartments have been labeled A, B, and C on the floor plan (See Figure 23). Today, doorways connect the apartments. During the period the building was used as apartments, there was only one doorway connecting two apartments. It connected Apartments A and B. Other doorways were put in after Max Smith sold the building in 1974.[19]

7

STAGE 2 – THE FIRST STONE ADDITION, APARTMENT-A

EXTERIOR FEATURES OF APARTMENT-A

Apartment-A was created from combining the 1870s balloon-framed structure with Clark's circa 1790 first stone addition. It fronts North Market Street. The exterior stonework of the circa 1790 stone addition is still intact with one exception, the chimney. Much of the original chimney is missing. Also missing are the original circa 1790 exterior wooden architectural features. The circa 1790 door and window jams, as well as the cornice, were likely replaced when the building was made into apartments in the 1870s. The exterior door on the North Market Street side of the building is contemporary. All the sash and glass in the windows dates to the 1870s, except those in the gable end of the attic. These appear to be original to the tavern period.

INTERIOR FIRST-FLOOR FEATURES OF APARTMENT-A

THE MAIN HALL (ROOM 101)

The main hall of the original tavern (room 101) is in the circa 1790 first stone addition (See Figure 24). Its size is 19 feet by 19 feet. All the floorboards appear to be original, except those used to replace the fireplace hearth.

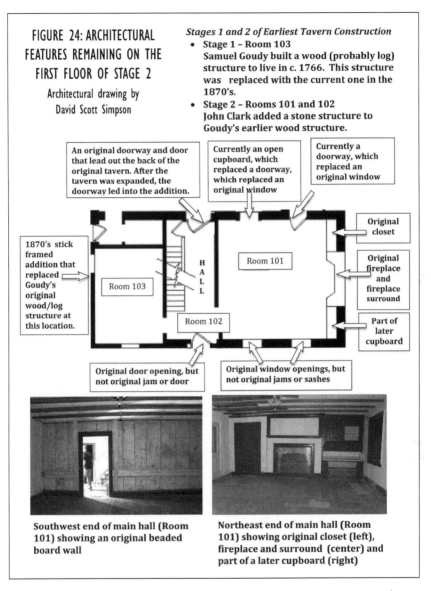

FIGURE 24: ARCHITECTURAL FEATURES REMAINING ON THE FIRST FLOOR OF STAGE 2

Architectural drawing by David Scott Simpson

Stages 1 and 2 of Earliest Tavern Construction
- Stage 1 – Room 103
  Samuel Goudy built a wood (probably log) structure to live in c. 1766. This structure was replaced with the current one in the 1870's.
- Stage 2 – Rooms 101 and 102
  John Clark added a stone structure to Goudy's earlier wood structure.

An original doorway and door that lead out the back of the original tavern. After the tavern was expanded, the doorway led into the addition.

Currently an open cupboard, which replaced a doorway, which replaced an original window

Currently a doorway, which replaced an original window

Original closet

1870's stick framed addition that replaced Goudy's original wood/log structure at this location.

Room 103

HALL

Room 101

Original fireplace and fireplace surround

Room 102

Part of later cupboard

Original door opening, but not original jam or door

Original window openings, but not original jams or sashes

Southwest end of main hall (Room 101) showing an original beaded board wall

Northeast end of main hall (Room 101) showing original closet (left), fireplace and surround (center) and part of a later cupboard (right)

At present, the original reciprocating sawn joists supporting the second floor are exposed in the ceiling of the main hall. Above them can be seen original second-floor floorboards in rooms 201 and 208.

Across the northeast end of the main hall is most of an original room-end. It consists of a stone chimney in the center with an original fireplace, surround, and over-mantle. To the left of the fireplace is the original closet. To the right of the fireplace are parts of a later built-in cupboard that, in more modern times, contained a kitchen sink. The cupboard and sink were put in during the apartment period.[1] Water-sawn joists are currently exposed in the main hall. They were originally covered with split-board lath and plastered. The outlines of the original lath and nail holes can be seen on the undersides of joists. Remnants of the plastered ceiling and lath can be found in the room-end's closet at the north corner of the room (See Figure 24). Early type-A machine-cut nails with hand-wrought heads hold up the remaining split lath in the closet. The nails and lath date the plastered ceiling to circa 1790–1820.[2]

The stone fireplace in the room is designed for heating. It is not a walk-in fireplace that would have been used for cooking. The fireplace surround and over-mantle have late 18th-century Georgian-style mold-ings. Other Georgian-style moldings are found on the casings or archi-traves around the two windows fronting North Market Street and the doorway into the stair hallway. The casing is composed of single-faced casing board with beaded edge. The beaded edge defines the inner openings of the windows and door. *Ovolo* or quarter round moldings were applied to the outer edges of the facing to give the casings a Georgian-style (See Figure 25).[3] The casings around the exterior doorway and the cupboard on the northwest wall are not original to the tavern period.

To the left of the fireplace is the previously mentioned original closet. In contemporary times, it was converted into a cupboard by adding shelves. From when it

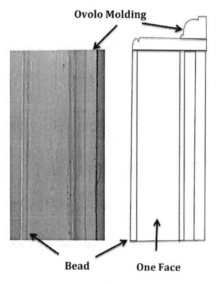

Ovolo Molding

Bead   **One Face**

FIGURE 25. 18TH-CENTURY STYLE ONE FACE, BEADED DOOR, AND WINDOW CASING was a closet, there are still hand-carved wooden pegs attached to the back wall.

The front of the closet (cupboard) has its original late 18th-century six-paneled door. It is attached to the original door-frame with two original cast-iron butt hinges. The hinges are fastened to the frame and the door with original hand-made screws. There is currently a later cast iron thumb latch on the exterior of the door. It replaced two earlier latches. The "ghost" or outline of the shape of the earliest handle reveals it was a hand-forged Suffolk or bean-style handle. An example of this type of handle was found in do-ing metal detecting sweeps on the north corner of the tavern's property (See Figure 26). Max, the last of the Smith family to

FIGURE 26: SUFFOLK THUMB LATCH ONCE USED IN THE TAVERN

own and live on the property, said he took doors with this type of handle from the tavern's attic and burned them on that north corner.[4]

On the opposite or southwest end of the room is an original wooden beaded-board wall (See Figure 24). Fortunately, board nailers were at-tached to the wall protecting it from the later wall built over it. As a result, the beaded-board wall still has its original gray paint. A nail in the beaded-board wall helped to identify the wall's date. Based on the nail, the wall was built sometime between 1780–1800.[5]

THE STAIR HALLWAY (ROOM 102)

The first-floor stair hallway is labeled room 102 on the floor plan (See Fig-ure 24). Its size is 8 feet by 19 feet. The hallway has its original floorboards and baseboards on the northwest and northeast sides (See Figure 27).

The northwest and southeast walls of the hall are plastered stone. The northeast wall that separates the stair hallway from the main hall has its original beaded-board wall under the plaster. The southwest wall and stairway were added in the 1870s. All of the parts appear to be from the

1870s except the stringer under where the balustrade was once located. Because it is beaded, it may have been reused from the tavern period.

The underlying structure of the stairs is framed with standardized lumber and is covered with sawn lath attached with cut nails. The original wall, which supported the original stairway, was probably made of logs and part of Goudy's original structure. When Goudy's log building collapsed, it likely took the wall and original stairway with it. Unfortunately, former vagrants stole the later 1870s Victorian cherry newel post and balustrade that replaced the tavern's original.[6]

In the doorjamb of the doorway leading from the stair hallway into Apartment-B is a hand-forged iron pintle. It, along with a missing pintle, was used for holding an exterior door with strap hinges. The doorway

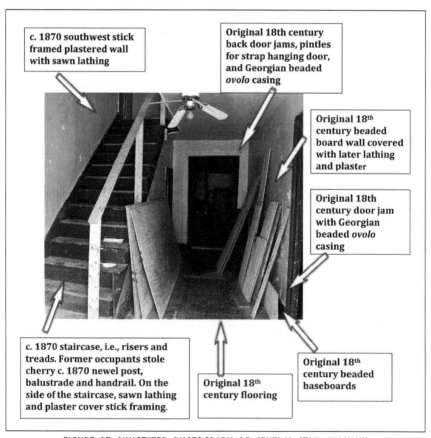

c. 1870 southwest stick framed plastered wall with sawn lathing

Original 18th century back door jams, pintles for strap hanging door, and Georgian beaded *ovolo* casing

Original 18th century beaded board wall covered with later lathing and plaster

Original 18th century door jam with Georgian beaded *ovolo* casing

c. 1870 staircase, i.e., risers and treads. Former occupants stole cherry c. 1870 newel post, balustrade and handrail. On the side of the staircase, sawn lathing and plaster cover stick framing.

Original 18th century flooring

Original 18th century beaded baseboards

FIGURE 27: ANNOTATED PHOTOGRAPH OF CENTRAL STAIR HALLWAY

would have been a backdoor for the tavern before Stage 3 was added. Although not currently hanging, an original exterior door still exists leaning against the wall in room 104 (See Figure 28). It is a six-paneled door with original red paint and hand-forged strap hinges (and fits the previously mentioned doorway). The door's original thumb latch is missing. The door was removed from the tavern sometime in the distant past. It was then given to the Duncannon Borough by one of its residents to be used in the tavern when the Borough bought the building.

In addition to the floorboards, some baseboards, the pintle and beaded-board wall, three of the five doorways in the stair hallway have 18th century, Georgian-style casings. Like the original window and door casings in the main hall, they are composed of single-faced

FIGURE 28: RED-PAINTED 18TH-CENTURY SIX-PANELED DOOR WITH STRAP HINGES

beaded-boards with *ovolo* moldings. One doorway with original casing goes into the main hall, another is the front doorway, and the third is what was once the previously discussed back doorway. Casings from a later period are around doorways that go into the 1870s addition and the basement.

APARTMENT-A'S BASEMENT AND CRAWLSPACE

Under the balloon-framed structure of Apartment-A and the first-floor stair hallway (room 102) is a basement. The basement under the hallway is original to the 1st stone addition (Stage2). When the balloon-framed structure was built, a basement was dug for it. The southwest wall of the original basement was torn down, and the balloon-framed basement joined with the original. The combined balloon-framed and Stage 2 basements originally had a dirt floor and were about 5' deep. Max Smith dug the cellar floors deeper. A subsequent owner had them cemented. There is only a crawlspace under the original main hall (room 101).[7]

Although the walls of the combined basements are constructed of stone, three of the tavern's original basement walls are discernable; southeast, northeast, and northwest. The southeast or North Market Street wall is slightly offset and defines the width of the original basement. The original walls are covered with a coat of cement for stabilization.[8] The walls were cemented after Max Smith sold the building in 1974.[9]

INTERIOR SECOND-FLOOR FEATURES OF APARTMENT-A

THE STAIR HALLWAY (ROOM 202)

At the top of the front stairs is a landing, room 202 (See Figures 29 & 30). The floorboards on the landing are likely original. The Victorian cherry balustrade that once went around the stairway opening was stolen

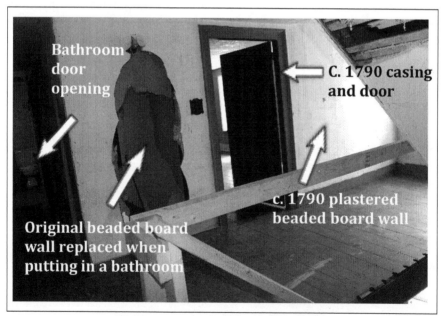

FIGURE 29: SECOND FLOOR STAIRWAY LANDING

by vagrants. The original 18th-century front window casing was also replaced.

Adjoining the northeast side of the stairway landing is a plastered wall with two doorways. One doorway goes into room 208, which was contemporaneously used as a bathroom. The other doorway goes into room 201, a bedroom (See Figures 29 & 30).

Max Smith stated when he took the plaster off the wall to open a doorway for the bathroom he was making out of room 208, he found overlapping, random width, vertical boards. He had to cut through these for the doorway.[10] These are likely the same type of 18th-century boards found between the stair hallway and the main hall on the first floor.

What Max did not know when he opened his bathroom doorway into room 208, was there was an original covered with plaster doorway and jamb just to the right of his (See Figure 30). This doorway was recently uncovered during restoration.

While the casing around Max Smith's bathroom doorway is contemporary, the casing around the doorway going into the bedroom (room 202) from the stair hallway is late 18th century (See Figure 30). The six-paneled door in this doorway is also original to the tavern period.

THE ORIGINAL MAIN BEDROOM AND ADJOINING BATH (ROOMS 201 AND 208)

On the southeast side of the stair hallway are two rooms, 201 and 208. In contemporary times, room 201 was a bedroom and 208 a bathroom, hall, and a closet. A late 18th-century beaded- board wall separates the two rooms (See Figure 30). The board wall has a doorway with late 18th-century casing and a late 18th-century six-paneled door. The baseboard at the base of the wall is from a later period. The original baseboard was likely replaced when the floor was refinished.

The beaded-board wall separating rooms 201 and 208 remains somewhat of a mystery. It divides what would have originally been a large fireplace-heated room into one heated and one unheated room. Because of this peculiarity and the wall's later baseboard, it was initially thought the wall might have been moved from another part of the tavern when

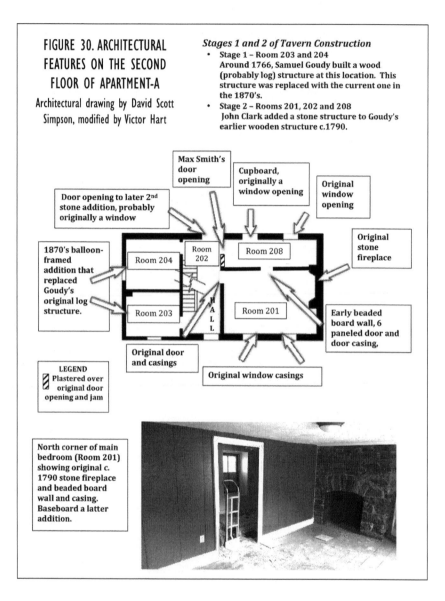

FIGURE 30. ARCHITECTURAL FEATURES ON THE SECOND FLOOR OF APARTMENT-A

Architectural drawing by David Scott Simpson, modified by Victor Hart

Stages 1 and 2 of Tavern Construction
- **Stage 1 – Room 203 and 204**
  Around 1766, Samuel Goudy built a wood (probably log) structure at this location. This structure was replaced with the current one in the 1870's.
- **Stage 2 – Rooms 201, 202 and 208**
  John Clark added a stone structure to Goudy's earlier wooden structure c.1790.

Max Smith's door opening

Cupboard, originally a window opening

Original window opening

Door opening to later 2nd stone addition, probably originally a window

1870's balloon-framed addition that replaced Goudy's original log structure.

Original stone fireplace

Room 204

Room 202

Room 208

Room 203

Room 201

HALL

Early beaded board wall, 6 paneled door and door casing,

Original door and casings

Original window casings

LEGEND
▨ Plastered over original door opening and jam

North corner of main bedroom (Room 201) showing original c. 1790 stone fireplace and beaded board wall and casing. Baseboard a latter addition.

the bathroom was created. Although covered with plaster, Max Smith stated the wall was already there when he constructed a hall, closet, and bathroom from room 208.[11]

Substantiating the late 18th-century date for the beaded-board wall is the recently uncovered doorway between the hallway (room 202) and bathroom (room 208). The doorway's late 18th-century casing matches that in the doorway of the beaded-board wall.

The layout of the bathroom's adjoining bedroom (room 201) replicates the main hall below it (room 101). If the beaded-board wall wasn't there, the room would be the same size and configuration as the main hall below. Also, like the main hall below, the room utilized the same chimney for its fireplace. Unlike the fireplace in the main hall, the bedroom's fireplace does not have a wooden fireplace surround and over-mantle.

In addition to its original fireplace and beaded-board wall, the bedroom has its original flooring, window and door casings, doors, and baseboards except on the beaded-board wall. Like the main hall below, it is believed the plastered wall separating the room from the hallway is constructed of beaded-boards under the plaster.

BEDROOMS IN THE BALLOON-FRAMED SECTION (ROOMS 203 AND 204)

Adjoining the stairway on the southwest side of the hall are doorways leading into rooms 203 and 204 (See Figure 30). These two bedrooms are part of the 1870s balloon-framed structure. Except for a few recycled late 18th-century architectural pieces used to help support the balloon-framing, the only possible early architectural feature is a door going into room 204. It appears to be an early six-paneled door moved from another location. Closer examination of the door is needed to determine if it dates to the late 18th century. The door going into room 203 is a later door constructed of earlier beaded boards.

8

STAGE 3 – THE SECOND STONE ADDITION, APARTMENTS B AND C

As previously mentioned, with the completion of a financially successful Philadelphia and Lancaster Turnpike in 1794, a wave of turnpike construction began in Pennsylvania.[1] These new and improved roads paved the way for increased numbers of settlers and businessmen heading west. In addition, the improved road system brought more of a new class of traveler to Clark's Ferry and Tavern, the upper class. These wealthier patrons now arrived in increasing numbers by stagecoach and carriage.

As such, by 1800, Clark's tavern not only needed to be made larger but also needed to contain private rooms for the upper class. Besides the usual public or bar room and communal bedrooms found in taverns, Clark's Tavern now needed a private dining room and private bedrooms for upper-class patrons who could afford them. These new customers included women.[2]

In addition, by 1800, the Clarks needed a larger tavern building to accommodate their family. By this time, the Clark children were growing into adulthood. The U.S. 1800 Census shows ten Clark family members living in the tavern at the time.[3]

Because of a need for a larger tavern with more specialized rooms, after Robert Clark bought his siblings' interests in the tavern in 1802 and paid off Mathias Flam for his Ferry Landing in 1804, it is thought

Robert built Stage 3 between 1805 and 1807. Stage 3 was the second stone addition and was added to the back of Stages 1 and 2. It gave the tavern an "L" shape (See Figure 22).

EXTERIOR FEATURES

CLARK STREET SIDE OF THE BUILDING

Like the first stone addition the second stone addition has three bays on each floor across the Clark's Street side of the building, but unlike the first addition, the doorway is the middle bay (See Figure 31).

On the exterior of the southeast or Clark Street side of the addition, the stonework is in relatively good condition. Like the other two sides of the addition, however, the window jambs, sash, and glass were later replacements. The original doorjamb and door on this side of the building were also replaced. Although having a cover, there is underneath it

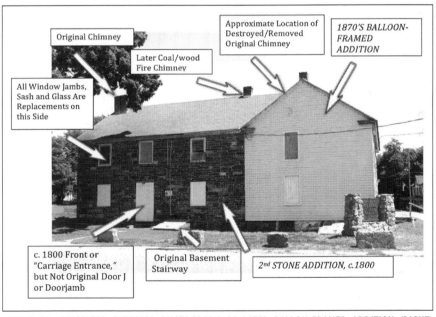

FIGURE 31: ANNOTATED EXTERIOR PHOTOGRAPH OF LATER BALLON-FRAMED ADDITION (RIGHT) AND SECOND STONE ADDITION (LEFT) — CLARK STREET SIDE OF THE TAVERN

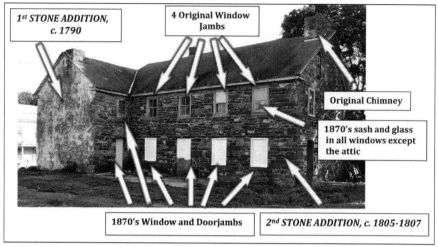

FIGURE 32: ANNOTATED EXTERIOR PHOTOGRAPH OF FIRST STONE ADDITION, c.1790 (LEFT) AND SECOND STONE ADDITION, c.1805–1807 (RIGHT) — MARGARETTA STREET SIDE OF THE TAVERN

a cemented basement stair. At the bottom of the stairs is an original basement doorway that is still operational.

MARGARETTA STREET SIDE OF THE BUILDING

The Margaretta Street side of the building has four bays on each floor with a doorway offset in the middle (See Figure 32). Today, there is only a chimney on the Apple Tree Alley end. Originally, there would have been another chimney on the North Market Street end of the building in Samuel Goudy's log structure. It is likely the chimney on the North Market Street end collapsed and/or was torn down as a result of the previously discussed three-day 1865 Flood.[4]

On the exterior of the northeast or Margaretta Street side of the addition, the circa 1805–1807 stonework is still intact. With the exception of four, second-floor mortice and tenon window jambs and a section of beaded-board fascia, all of the circa 1805–1807 exterior wooden architectural features have been replaced. The original doorjamb and most window jambs were likely replaced when the building was remodeled in the 1870s. The exterior door is also from a later period. Steps leading to an original basement doorway were cemented over when a patio was laid.

APPLE TREE ALLEY STREET SIDE OF THE BUILDING

On the exterior of the northwest or Apple Tree Alley end of the addition, the stonework appears in good shape except for the chimney. The chimney has some structural problems above the roofline. Window jambs, sash, and glass on this end of the building were replaced in the 1870s. It is believed the door and doorway on this end of the building were put in when the building was converted to apartments. It is thought that there was originally a window where the doorway is now located.

FIGURE 33: APPLE TREE ALLEY SIDE OF THE TAVERN

BASIC APARTMENT FLOOR PLANS

The basic floor plans of all three apartments, A, B, and C, date to the 1870s (See Figure 23). Apartment-A was made from combining the first stone addition with the balloon-framed structure that replaced Goudy's original log house. Apartments B and C were constructed by dividing the second stone addition into two apartments.

When the Smiths owned the building, each of the three apartments had a living room and kitchen on the first floor. The living room faced northwest or Clark Street and the kitchen northeast or Margaretta Street. On the first floor of each apartment was a stairway to a second floor and under it, a stairway to a basement.

On the second floor of each apartment, the floor was divided so that each apartment originally had two bedrooms. Later the bedroom in each apartment on the Margaretta Street side of the building was divided into a bath, small hallway, and smaller bedroom when water and sanitation became available. Only Apartments A and C originally had stairways to the second floor and basement. New second floor and basement stairways had to be built for Apartment-B. Only Apartments A and C had stairways to the attic. To create separate apartments from the tavern's connected rooms, several of the original interior doorways were closed and plastered over. Additionally, new walls with new doorways were constructed.[5] Some of the floorboards and baseboards were also replaced.

STAGE 3'S FIRST-FLOOR ROOMS

ORIGINAL PUBLIC OR BAR ROOM (ROOM 104) – APARTMENT-B'S KITCHEN

In Stages 1 and 2 of the tavern, it is believed the public or bar room was in Goudy's original log structure. Once the second stone addition was built, it is believed the public or bar room was in what later became Apartment-B's kitchen, room 104 (See Figure 35). This belief is based on the location of the kitchen's exterior doorway.

The public or bar room would have been the most used room in the tavern and had the most used exterior doorway. Today the exterior doorway of the former kitchen faces Margaretta Street. During the tavern period, the doorway opened to the tavern's heavily used wagon yard, making it the most used.

The geography of the tavern property dictates the wagon yard was on the Margaretta Street side of the building. The large yard was restricted from being on the southeast or what is today the North Market Street side of the tavern because of the Susquehanna River and its floodplain. It wouldn't have been on the southwest or Clark Street side of the tavern because of Clark's Run. And finally, a steeply sloped hill and likely apple orchard were on what is today the northwest or Apple Tree Alley side of the tavern. The only side of the tavern with enough dry level land for the large, heavily used wagon yard was the southeast or what is today the Margaretta Street side of the tavern. Because of its location and former use, the exterior doorway in room 104 was labeled the "Wagoner's Entrance" on the proposed circa 1805–1807 Floor Plan (See Figure 36). The only other exterior doorway leading to the location of the wagon yard is in Apartment-A's kitchen, room 101. This doorway was constructed during the Apartment Period.

While most common travelers would have come into the tavern using the public or bar room door facing the wagon yard, wealthy upper-class patrons arriving in carriages would have likely been left off at the front entrance. The first stone addition's front entryway on North Market Street was likely used for this purpose. As such, it was labeled the "Carriage Entrance" on the proposed floor plan (See Figure 36). Having left off their passengers at the front entrance, carriage drivers would have driven their vehicles around to the wagon yard where they would have watered, fed, and perhaps stabled their horses. Drivers would then have entered the tavern's public or bar room through the "Wagoner's Entrance."

When converting what is believed to have been the public or bar room into Apartment-B's kitchen, room 104, both moderate and major changes were made to the room (See Figures 34 & 35). Moderate changes consisted of adding appliances and cupboards. Cupboards were added to

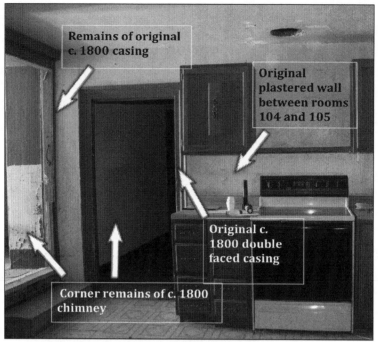

Remains of original
c. 1800 casing

Original
plastered wall
between rooms
104 and 105

Original c.
1800 double
faced casing

Corner remains of c. 1800
chimney

FIGURE 34: WALL DIVIDING APARTMENT-B'S KITCHEN (ROOM 104)
AND LIVING ROOM (ROOM 105)

a wall that separates the kitchen from what was once the apartment's living room (room 105).

Although the appliances and cupboards are from a later period, the wall itself is original to the tavern period. Its framework is constructed of rough-cut wooden studs. The studs were cut from wide wooden boards. Over these were nailed hand-riven lath, which was covered with plaster.

In addition to the wall being original to the tavern period, the current doorway in the wall between rooms 104 and 105 is original, as are the Georgian-style casings around it (See Figure 34).

Another minor architectural change in the room is a closed doorway between rooms 104 and 101 (See Figure 36). This doorway was likely a window during Stage 2 of the tavern. When Stage 3, the second stone addition, was added, it is thought the window was converted into a doorway. The doorway led from the public or bar room (room 104) into the first stone addition's main hall (room 101). An architectural "ghost" or

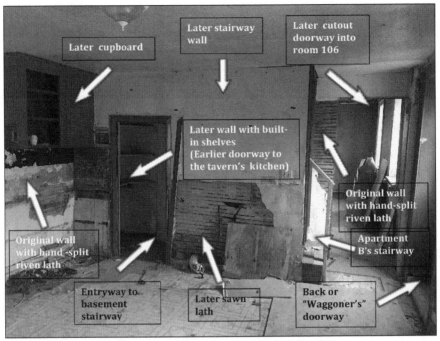

FIGURE 35: APARTMENT-B'S 1870s STAIRWAY WALL

outline on the beaded-board wall of the hall indicates the door entered into a bar cage in the room (See Figure 36). When the doorway was closed, space in the doorway was left in room 101 to make a cupboard. On the back wall on the inside of the cupboard is inscribed in plasterer, "J. W. Smith, 4/6/19"[6] J. W. Smith was Max Smith's father, Joseph. By trade, he was a "plasterer & cement man."[7] The doorway was closed by him in 1919.

In addition to minor changes made in Apartment-B's Kitchen, several major changes were also made. As previously mentioned, a new stairway to the second floor and one to the basement were constructed in the 1870s (See Figure 35). The basement stairs were constructed under the second-floor stairs. The second floor and basement stairways were built along the northwest wall of the room. The wall separates room 105 from room 106. This wall was original to the tavern. Like the wall between rooms 104 and 105, this wall still has some of its original rough-cut wooden studs, hand-wrought nails, hand-split lath, and plaster.

In constructing the second floor and basement stairways for Apartment-B, builders covered over two of the tavern's original interior doorways. One of the doorways was in the center of the wall that separates rooms 104 and 106. It was closed when the second-floor stairway and basement stairway beneath it were built. The doorway's original doorjamb can be seen in room 106, on the other side of the stairway wall (See Figure 39).

The current doorway in the wall separating rooms 104 and 106 was cut through the original wooden and plastered wall when the building was converted from apartments to a single-family dwelling.

The second original blocked doorway is in the wall at the back of the cupboard on the basement stairway's landing. The landing is under the second-floor stairway (See Figure 36). The closed doorway was originally part of a passageway that went from the tavern's original kitchen, room 107, to the public or bar room, room 104. The passageway would have been used for transporting food from the kitchen to patrons in the public or bar room and drinks from the basement to the bar cage that was built against the wall (See Figure 36). The original basement stairway (now closed off) was under the second-floor stairway in room 107.

Today in room 104, there are still original circa 1805–1807 Georgian-style casings around the doorway to the former wagon yard, to room 102, and to room 105 (See Figure 35). There is also original casing around the window in room 104. The casings around the doorway to the basement's landing and the one into room 106 are from a later period. Beaded baseboards on the northeast and southeast walls are original; others are not. It is believed the flooring in the room is original, but it is covered with linoleum. One other original architectural feature is a reused part of a chair rail that holds up a shelf in the basement landing's cupboard.

Heat in the public or bar room was provided by an iron stove that stood along the wall that separates the room from room 105 (See Figure 36). It was vented by a pipe that went to a brick chimney on the second floor in room 205.

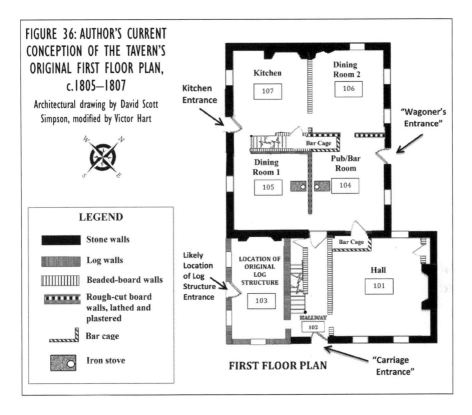

FIGURE 36: AUTHOR'S CURRENT CONCEPTION OF THE TAVERN'S ORIGINAL FIRST FLOOR PLAN, c.1805–1807

Architectural drawing by David Scott Simpson, modified by Victor Hart

LEGEND

■ Stone walls
▨ Log walls
▥ Beaded-board walls
⸬ Rough-cut board walls, lathed and plastered
⌐ Bar cage
◨ Iron stove

Kitchen Entrance

Kitchen 107

Dining Room 2 106

"Wagoner's Entrance"

Bar Cage

Dining Room 1 105

Pub/Bar Room 104

Likely Location of Log Structure Entrance

LOCATION OF ORIGINAL LOG STRUCTURE 103

Bar Cage

Hall 101

HALLWAY 102

FIRST FLOOR PLAN

"Carriage Entrance"

ORIGINAL DINING ROOM (ROOM 105) – APARTMENT-B'S LIVING ROOM

Apartment-B's living room was one of the tavern's two dining rooms. It is labeled Dining Room 1 in Figure 36. The two-faced Georgian-style casing around the room's two open doorways (and one that is closed) indicates it was the most important room in the building. It is the only room in the tavern with this elaborate type of door casing. As such, it is thought to have been reserved for the Clark family and wealthier guests.

Another indication that room 105 was the dining room is its location next to what was the 2nd addition's kitchen (room 107). The original kitchen for Stages 1 and 2 of the tavern was in Goudy's original log house.

When constructing the 2nd addition of the tavern, a doorway was created in the wall separating the kitchen and the dining room. It allowed food to be easily taken from the kitchen into the adjoining dining room

(See Figure 36). When Apartments B and C were constructed, the doorway was closed and remains so today. The original doorjamb, with its original casing, still lies beneath the more modern plastered wall. Apart from the plastered shut doorway, the wall separating the original dining room from the kitchen is original. It is constructed of plaster applied to hand-split lath, which is attached with hand-forged nails to split boards.

The casing around the only window in room 205 is original, as are three of the room's beaded baseboards.

Dining room 1 was heated by an iron stove that stood next to the wall separating it from the public or bar room. Like the public or bar room, the stove's pipe vented to the brick chimney in room 205 above it.

THE TAVERN'S KITCHEN (ROOM 107) – APARTMENT-C'S LIVING ROOM

The front doorway to Apartment-C faces northwest or Clark Street. During the Apartment Period, it would have been the apartment's front door into its living room. During the earlier tavern period, it was an exterior doorway for the tavern's kitchen, likely leading to a springhouse and bake oven. Since Clark's Run is today under the driveway of 3Bs Ice Cream Shop on the other side of Clark Street, the remains of the structures are likely to be under Clark Street, if they still exist.

Room 107 has more original architectural features than any other room in Apartment-B or C. After stepping through the Clark Street doorway, an original kitchen fireplace is to the left, and a stairway and its landing are to the right. The previously mentioned closed doorway from the kitchen to the dining room is under the plaster on the North Market Street side of the landing. (See Figure 37).

Except for the stringers, the current stairway is not original. Based on the Craftsman style of the balustrade, the original balustrade, treads and risers were replaced in the early 1900's. The date of the remodeling is reinforced by an inscription in plaster under the stringers. The plaster is inscribed "J.W. Smith 7/24/1924. This was Joseph Smith, Max Smith's father.

At the top of the current stairway is a landing that appears to be original. At the front of the landing is an original wall made of hand-split lath attached with hand-forged nails to split boards. To the right on the landing is a doorway that leads into room 205. The doorway is original to the tavern period. To the left on the landing is another doorway with original casings on both sides.

Under the stairway to the second floor is a closet (See Figure 37). The author believes the closet was added during the apartment period and originally the area under the stairway was open. Inside the closet, there is a wall on the left-hand side as you enter. It was likely constructed when the closet was built. The wall is the size of a door and has circa 1805–1807 door casing around it. The wall blocks what was the previously-mentioned original passageway between the tavern's kitchen, (room 107) and the bar cage in the public or bar room (room 104) (See Figure 36).

As you enter the closet, in front of you are built-in shelves from a later period. These are attached, however, to an original beaded-board wall. These boards run the width of the wall under the stairs. Like the other original boards in the tavern, they are attached vertically. Further inspection of the wall above the second floor stairway showed that the beaded-board wall continues to the third floor.

Opposite this wall, under the second-floor stairway, is another beaded-board wall to which the stairway is attached. It separates the in-side of the closet from the original kitchen. Instead of running vertically, however, the boards in the wall run horizontally, indicating they had been reused when the present stairway was constructed. Examination of the still attached beaded-boards covering the risers and treads under the top of the stairway show they were taken from the uncovered risers and treads at the bottom of the stairway.

On the floor under the second-floor stairs is a boarded-shut open-ing that once contained the 2nd addition's original basement stairway (See Figure 37). The opening was boarded shut when the stairway was removed after the apartment period. During the apartment period, the stairway was used by Apartment-C to access the basement. At that time, a wall divided the basement into two parts. Apartment-C used one half, while Apartment-B used the other half. Each apartment had its own set of stairs to its half of the basement.[8]

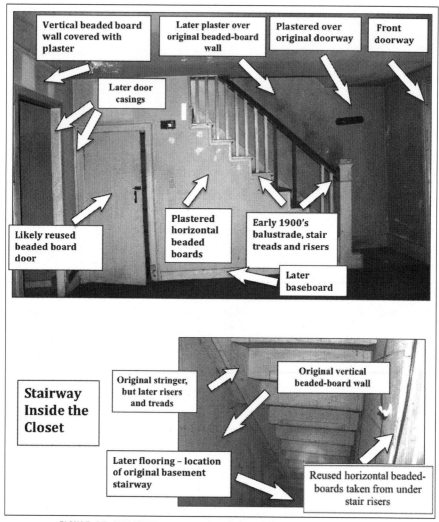

FIGURE 37: ANNOTATED PHOTOGRAPH OF EARLY 1900s STAIRWAY AND CLOSET ENTRANCE (ROOM 107)

In room 107, the most predominant architectural feature is its cooking fireplace on the Apple Tree Alley side of the room (See Figure 38). The fireplace is in its original condition, with three exceptions. First, the hearth in front of the fireplace was replaced with wood flooring. Second, in more recent times, holes were drilled in the fireplace's wooden lintel.

And third, the back of the fireplace was coated with cement. It should be noted that Joseph Smith also left his "calling card" in the cement on the back of the fireplace. Inscribed in cement are the initials and date, "J.W.S. 1924." Joseph must have been busy that year.

The floors of the tavern's former kitchen appear to be original but are currently covered with linoleum. The casing around the window in the room is original. The window sash and glass, however, are from the 1870s. Likewise, the room's baseboards are from a later period.

Separating the original kitchen (room 107) from adjoining room 106 is an original beaded-board wall (See Figure 38). A pass-through was cut out of the beaded-board wall during the apartment time period. The doorway through the wall between the kitchen and dining room 2 (room 106) dates to the tavern time period.

DINING ROOM 2 (ROOM 106) – APARTMENT-C'S KITCHEN

On the northeast side of room 107's beaded-board wall is Room 106. It was remodeled to become a kitchen for Apartment-C. During the tavern period, it is thought the room was used as a second dining room. As

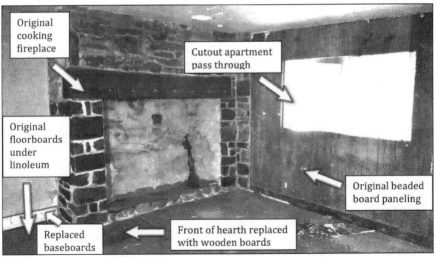

Original cooking fireplace

Cutout apartment pass through

Original floorboards under linoleum

Original beaded board paneling

Replaced baseboards

Front of hearth replaced with wooden boards

FIGURE 38: NORTH CORNER OF THE SECOND STONE ADDITION'S KITCHEN WITH COOKING FIREPLACE AND BEADED-BOARD WALL (ROOM 107)

such, it is identified as Dining Room 2 (See Figure 36). Because of the more elaborate two-faced door casings around the doorways to Dining Room 1 and because of its location at the bottom of the stairway, it is hypothesized that Dining Room 1 was used by the Clarks and their wealthier customers and Dining Room 2 by everyone else.

In the west corner of the dining room is a fireplace. In converting the room into Apartment-C's kitchen, the fireplace was closed and covered with a built-in cupboard. The cupboard has now been taken out, exposing the fireplace.

In the center of the southeast wall of the room is the previously discussed closed circa1805–1807 doorway between rooms 106 and 104 (See Figure 39). The wall and closed doorway are original to the tavern period. After taking off later lath and plaster from the wall, supports for an original wall and the doorjamb were found underneath. The original wall studs outside the doorjamb are hand-cut from wide wooden boards. Hand-split lath was nailed to the studs and plaster applied to them. The doorway was closed when Apartment-B's second floor and basement stairways were built. During the Apartment Period, there was no doorway between Apartments B and C. The current doorway between the apartments was cut through later when the building was used as a private dwelling.

On the northeast or Apple Tree Alley side of the room, there is an exterior doorway. It is not clear if the doorway was present during the tavern period. It seems likely it was put in for use by Apartment-C to gain access to its privy. It is thought the doorway was a window during the tavern period. The door in the doorway is from a later period.

The window casings around the two windows in the room are original to the tavern period. The window sash and glass are from the 1870s. The original baseboards have been replaced.

Unfortunately, because of water damage, some of the original floorboards and log joists holding them up are decayed and in a somewhat dangerous condition. For safety purposes, the floors have been temporarily covered with sheets of plywood. Repairing/replacing the joists and floors should be a top priority during the restoration of the building.

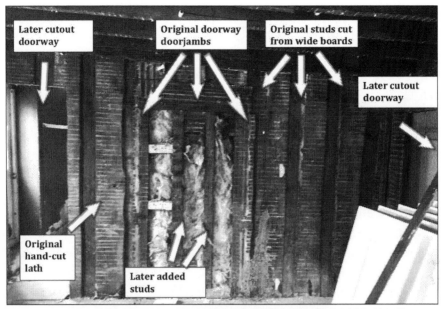

FIGURE 39: ORIGINAL WALL AND CLOSED DOORWAY SEPARATING ROOM 106 IN APARTMENT-C AND APARTMENT-B'S 1870s STAIRWAY

STAGE 3'S SECOND-FLOOR ROOMS

When the tavern's second stone addition was converted into Apartments B and C, the four bedrooms on the second-floor reflected the location and size of the rooms beneath them. Like the first floor, each apartment on the second floor had two rooms. One was on the Clark Street side of the building and one on the Margaretta Street side. Each apartment had its own second-floor stairway. Apartment-B's was created for it in the 1870s. Apartment-C's was the 2nd stone addition's only known original stairway.

After sewage and water services became available, Max Smith divided the 2nd floor Margaretta Street bedrooms in Apartment-B and Apartment-C into a bath with a cupboard, a short hallway, and a smaller bedroom. In addition, a landing for the newly constructed second-floor stairway was built for Apartment-B (See Figure 40).

APARTMENT-B'S ORIGINAL CLARK STREET BEDROOM (ROOM 205)

Except for creating a small walk-through closet, the size and shape of room 205 appears to be basically the same as it was during the tavern period (See Figure 40). Today there are two doors leading from the room into an adjoining hallway (room 206). These doors were put in during the apartment period and were not there when the building was a tavern. During the tavern period, there were only two entryways into the room. One was from the second-floor stairway and the other was from the attic stairway. Both are on the Apple Tree Alley side of the room.

Like the dining room below it, the original southwest wall of the room was composed mostly of a large chimney. To heat Samuel Goudy's original log house (the first stage of the tavern), a fireplace chimney was along the North Market Street end of the room. When the "Old Timer" stated that farmer, Christ Klinepeter, "stored some hay on the (open) second floor" of the building and a cat "jumped out onto the roof through the hole left by the chimney," he was referring to room 205.[9] Room 205 was heated with an iron stove that was vented by a brick chimney in the room.

In room 205, the casing around the one window in the room and the floorboards appear original to the tavern period. Also original to the tavern period are the beaded-board walls under the plastered walls on the Apple Tree Alley side of the room. There is currently a closed-off doorway going through the beaded board wall. The doorway leads to the attic's landing and stairway and through to room 107. Not original in the room are the casings around the four doorways, doors in two of them, the baseboards, and the window sash and glass. Along the northwest wall, there is a small area of floorboards that was cut out for some unknown reason and later repaired with the same boards.

APARTMENT-B'S ORIGINAL MARGARETTA STREET BEDROOM (ROOMS 206, 209, AND 210)

The room that was Apartment-B's original Margaretta Street side bedroom was the most remodeled area in the Stage 3 addition. When it was first converted to an apartment, a stairway was added to the second floor into the room (See Figure 40). The area for the current stairway and landing was cut from the original Margaretta Street side bedroom. With the advent of modern sewage and plumbing, Max Smith constructed walls dividing the bedroom into a bath (room 210), a small bedroom (room 209), and hall (room 206). In making all the alterations, all the observable circa 1805–1807 architectural features were removed and replaced except for the casing around the window in room 210. Features replaced included window sash and glass, doorway casings, doors, flooring, and baseboards.

It is likely the wall between rooms 210 in Apartment-B and 211 in Apartment-C is original. It is located above the previously discussed original wall on the first floor. If the wall is original, like the wall beneath it, it likely had a doorway in the center of it. The doorway would have been closed when the apartments were built. Further examination is needed to determine if there is a closed doorway.

APARTMENT-C'S ORIGINAL CLARK STREET BEDROOM (ROOM 207)

The Clark Street bedroom in Apartment-C is the least remodeled bedroom on the second floor of the 2nd stone addition. The size and shape have not been altered in any way (See Figure 40). The window casing, baseboards, and floors appear to be original to the tavern period. The doorways between it and room 211, Apartment-B's bath, as well as the one between it and the second-floor stairway landing have their original Georgian-style casing.

The doorway between 207 and bedroom 212 is not original to the tavern. When the Margaretta Street bedroom was divided into a bath, small hall, closet, and bedroom, a doorway was cut through an original wall into room 212. The casing around both sides of the doorway is from a later period. Like the rest of the tavern, the window sash and glass in the windows are also from a later period.

There is a large original chimney along the northwest wall of the room. It once vented the corner fireplace in adjacent room 212. It also vented the cooking fireplace in room 107 and the corner fireplace in room 106 on the first floor. The chimney appears to be in good condition in this room. No fireplace was built into the chimney in this room. When the author asked Max Smith how many flues were in the chimney, he stated three.[10] The cooking fireplace in room 107 and the corner fireplaces in rooms 106 and 212 accounts for these three flues. In addition, none of the floorboards in front of the chimney have been replaced,

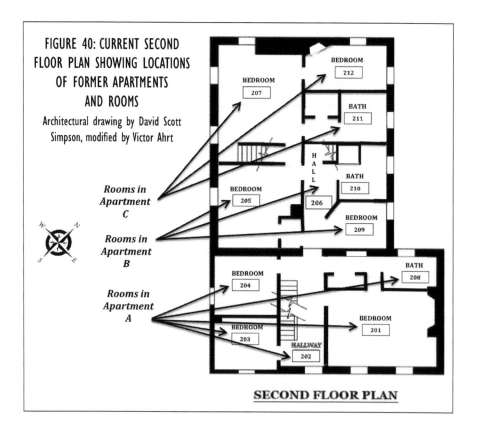

FIGURE 40: CURRENT SECOND FLOOR PLAN SHOWING LOCATIONS OF FORMER APARTMENTS AND ROOMS

Architectural drawing by David Scott Simpson, modified by Victor Ahrt

Rooms in Apartment C

Rooms in Apartment B

Rooms in Apartment A

BEDROOM 212

BEDROOM 207

BATH 211

HALL

BATH 210

BEDROOM 205

206

BEDROOM 209

BATH 208

BEDROOM 204

BEDROOM 203

BEDROOM 201

HALLWAY 202

SECOND FLOOR PLAN

indicating there had never been a fireplace hearth. Heat for the room was acquired through an iron grate that opened to the kitchen below it.

At the south corner of room 207 is a doorway leading to a landing for the attic stairway (See Figure 40). Part of the original doorway casing appears to be around the doorway opening, but some was removed when the drywall was later added.

The attic stairway and landing are original to the tavern period. Originally, the landing appears to have been accessed from doorways in both rooms 205 and 207. The walls going up the sides of the stairway are paneled with vertical beaded-boards. Further examination of the stairway wall in room 205 is needed to see if the stairway's beaded-board wall found in room 207 is also present in room 205. It is most likely present.

Besides the original beaded-board walls, another interesting architectural feature in the stairway is an original chair rail. It is attached to the plastered stone wall of the landing and was likely placed there to protect the plastered wall when moving objects to the attic.

APARTMENT-C'S ORIGINAL MARGARETTA STREET BEDROOM (ROOMS 211 AND 212)

When Apartment-C was first created, there would have been a second bedroom on the northeast or Margaretta Street side of the building. When plumbing and water services became available, walls were constructed to divide the bedroom. The room was divided into a bathroom with a short hall and closet (room 211) and a small bedroom or dressing room (room 212) (See Figure 40). The doorway between the Clark Street bedroom into the bathroom is original to the tavern period. It still has its Georgian-style casings on both sides. Based on the casing around the doorway between rooms 207 and room 212, the doorway was added when the small room was created for the apartment.

There are still some architectural features remaining from the tavern period in rooms 211 and 212. Besides the previously mentioned door casing, a recently discovered corner fireplace was uncovered in the west corner of room 212. Unfortunately, it appears the large stone lintel going across the fireplace opening is cracked. At some date, the fireplace opening was filled with brick to help to support the lintel and close off the fireplace opening. The fireplace hearth was replaced with boards.

It is likely the floorboards in room 211 or 212 are original to the tavern period, but they are currently covered with carpet or linoleum. There may be a few of the tavern's original baseboards still present in room 212, but these are covered with heating elements. Those not covered in either room are from a later period.

The window casings in both rooms 211 and 212 are original to the tavern, but the sash and glass in them are from the 1870s.

Since the original floor plan of the second floor reflects that of the first floor, the wall between rooms 211 and 212 was constructed when the apartments were made. As previously mentioned, it is believed the wall between 211 and 210 was original to the addition.

STAGE 3'S BASEMENT AND CRAWLSPACES

Although extensively modified, Apartment-C has an original basement under about one-half of it. As previously mentioned, the apartment's basement was accessed originally from a stairway under the second-floor stairway in room 107. At some point after the apartment period, the stairway was removed, and its opening closed. The basement's current stairway opening is located under the second-floor stairway in room 104, Apartment-B. This stairway was created in the 1870s when the apartments were constructed. The stairs in the stairway are no longer present. They were removed, and today a ladder is needed to gain access to the basement.

Apartment-C only has half a basement. It is located under the southeast half of the apartment. It is about 10' wide and extends about 28' from Clark Street to Margaretta Street. During the apartment period, a now missing wall divided the basement. With the basement divided, both Apartments B and C had their own interior stairway. They also each had an exterior door and stairway.[11] The exterior door and stairway on the Clark Street side of the basement are still functional, but the Margaretta Street side has been blocked off at ground level by a cement patio.

A crawlspace is located under the northwest half of the Apartment-C. The chimney base for the first-floor's cooking fireplace in room 107 and corner fireplace in room 106, as well as the second-floor corner fireplace in room 212, is in this crawlspace. Apartment-B only has a crawlspace under it.

Both the crawlspace and basement under Apartment-B and Apartment-C have first-floor joists made of hand-hewn logs with bark on their sides. Unfortunately, extensive water damage was done to some of the joists, and they will need additional support.

9

SUMMARY AND CONCLUSION OF THE TAVERN'S CONSTRUCTION

In 1787, when John Clark bought the tavern property named "Silver Spring" from Samuel Goudy and his wife Sara, it had two log houses on it. In 1788, when John and his oldest son Daniel started Clark's Ferry across the Susquehanna River, one of these buildings was likely used as an unlicensed tavern serving food and drink to travelers. In 1865, a devastating flood probably destroyed this log portion of the tavern. None of Stage 1, Goudy's log house, exists today. It was replaced in the 1870s with the current balloon-framed structure.

The first stone addition, Stage 2 of the tavern, was added onto Goudy's log building circa 1790. The vertically sawn lumber used in building the interior of the stone addition was not locally available until 1789. In addition, the tavern was first licensed in 1790 to Daniel Clark.

The 1st stone addition has a stair hallway, stairway, and main hall on the first floor and a stair hallway and two bedrooms on the second. Of the two stone additions, the 1st has been changed the least from the tavern period. When the tavern building was remodeled in the 1870s into apartments, it, along with the balloon-framed structure attached to it, was made into Apartment-A.

No historic date has been uncovered for the construction of Stage 3, the 2nd stone addition of the tavern. The U.S. Direct Tax of 1798 tells us it was not in existence that year. Based on Robert Clark's finances, the style of the building, its architectural features, construction, and building materials, a date of circa 1805–1807 has been ascribed to the building.

By 1805 Robert Clark had taken complete ownership of the tavern and ferry and paid off his debt to Mathias Flam for the purchase of Flam's Ferry Landing in Dauphin County. Because of improved road conditions, his ferry and tavern now served increasing numbers of their regular types of customers. In addition, stagecoaches and carriages started to cross on the ferry and stop at the tavern. They carried a new wealthier, upper-class customer. As a result, when Robert built the 2nd stone addition, it not only needed to be larger but required new types of facilities such as a dining room and private sleeping quarters to accommodate its new upper-class clientele, including women.

After Robert Clark's death, his wife Margaretta married Zachariah Rice. Together, they sold the dilapidated tavern and its property in 1869 to William King, Joseph Swartz, and John Shively. These three men bought the tavern and 200 acres to subdivide the acreage into housing lots they called Baskinsville. In 1875, three of these lots and a dilapidated tavern building were sold to David and Enos Smith. David and his brother Enos, then built a two-story, balloon-framed structure to replace Samuel Goudy's log house. Together, the combined balloon-framed structure and two stone additions were to be used as four apartments.

In 1880, for unknown reasons, David and Enos were forced to sell the tavern and its lots at a sheriff sale. At the sale, Enos rebought the tavern and lots with Michael Smith, either his brother or father. They converted the four apartments into three. The combined balloon-framed structure and first stone addition on North Market Street became one apartment. Because of the size of the second stone addition and the configuration of its rooms, the second stone addition was converted into two apartments.

Enos' grandson was Max Smith. Max was the last of three generations of the Smith family to own and live in the apartments. The Smiths always lived in the North Market Street apartment. Max was responsible for upgrading heating systems and installing plumbing in the apartments.

When Max sold the tavern and the accompanying lots in 1974, the subsequent owners converted the apartments into a single-family dwelling and attempted to restore some of the rooms to their original condition. Over time, the building went through a series of owners, and the condition of the building deteriorated. Eventually, vagrants began living in the building and ransacked it. The owners made attempts to sell the building, but without success. The building continued to deteriorate to an unsafe condition. To save the building from the wrecking ball, the Borough of Duncannon bought the building in 2012. In 2015, because of a lack of funding to repair and restore the tavern, its ownership was transferred to the Historical Society of Perry County, who presently owns it. The Historical Society is currently removing many of the building's later architectural features and raising money for the building's restoration.

Appendix A

Survey Road Maps Drawn by Robert Clark

MAP 1: JUNE 6, 1804, ROAD DRAFT FROM BRIGHTFIELD'S RUN NEAR MCGINNES'
SAWMILL TO (MARY) CLARK'S FERRY ON THE SUSQUEHANNA[1]

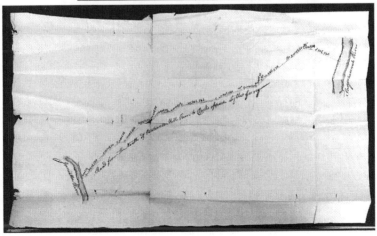

MAP 2: MARCH 11, 1812, ROAD DRAFT FROM THE GREAT ROAD THAT LEADS FROM HARRISBURG TO HUNTINGDON AND INTERSECTS THE GREAT ROAD FROM CLARK'S FERRY TO SHERMAN'S VALLEY[2]

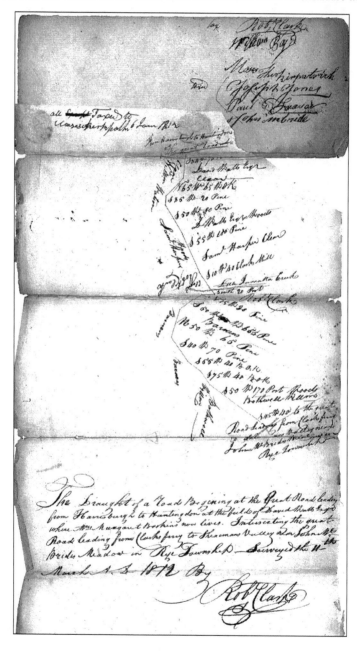

MAP 3: DECEMBER 27, 1815, PRELIMINARY ROAD DRAFT FROM SHEEP ISLAND TO CLARK'S FERRY[3]

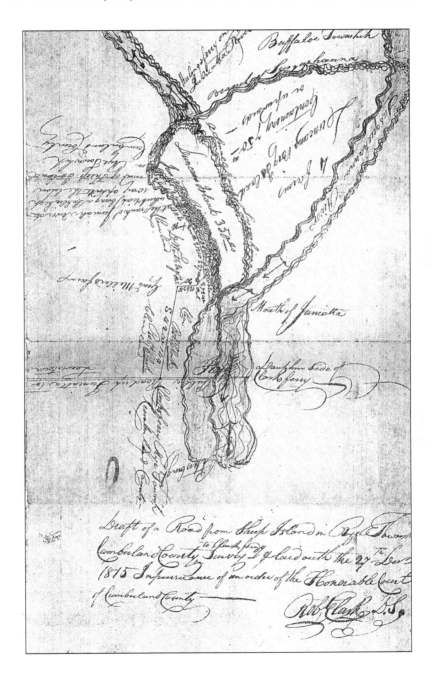

MAP 4: MAY 28, 1816, FINAL ROAD DRAFT FROM SHEEP ISLAND TO CLARK'S FERRY[4]

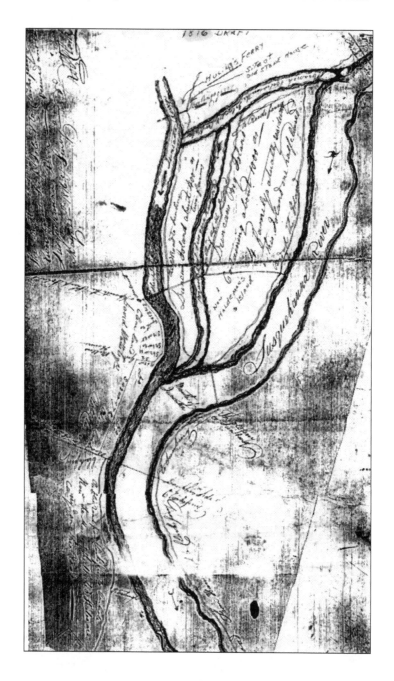

MAP 5: OCTOBER 14, 1818, ROAD DRAFT OF THE JUNCTION OF THE PUBLIC ROADS LEADING UP THE JUNIATA RIVER TO CLARK'S MILL[5]

MAP 6: MARCH 26 & 27, 1819, ROAD DRAFT FROM CLARK'S FERRY TO A POINT ON THE JUNIATA RIVER ACROSS FROM SHEEP ISLAND[6]

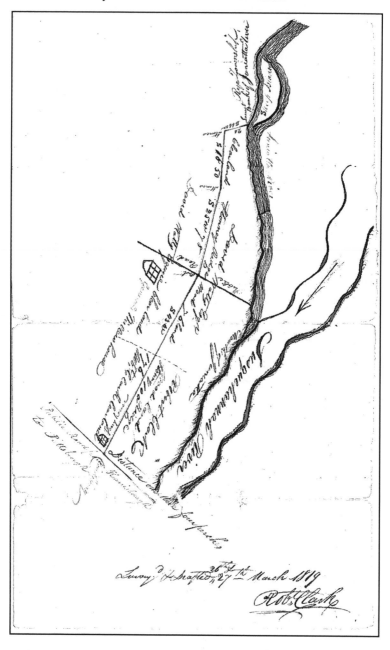

MAP 7: APRIL 30, 1824, ROAD VIEWING FOR THE GREAT NORTHERN TURNPIKE ROAD NEAR THE MOUTH OF THE JUNIATA RIVER TO NEAR NEW BERRY'S FALLS[7]

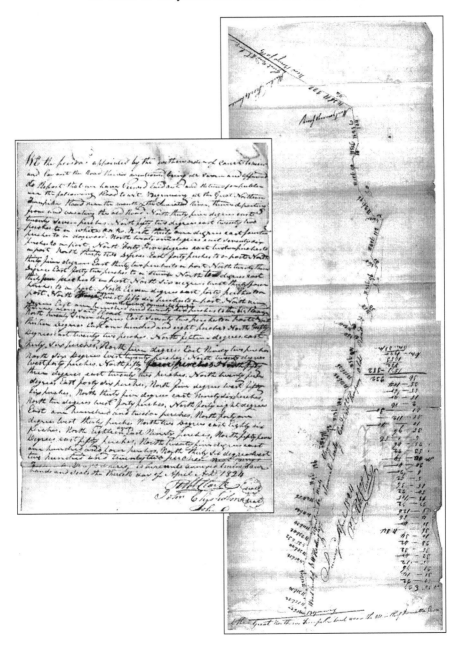

APPENDIX B

CLARK TIMELINE

PRE-FERRY AND TAVERN (1766–1787)

1766 Samuel Goudy established a homestead in Rye Township, Cumberland County, Pennsylvania, that later became the location for John Clark's tavern and ferry landing.

1768 Samuel Goudy surveyed 200 acres (actually 215 acres) of his homestead.

1774 Samuel Goudy warranted his homestead as "Silver Spring."

1785 Samuel Goudy advertised "Silver Spring" for sale in the Carlisle *Gazette.*

1786 Having emigrated from Scotland, Daniel Clark was taxed in Cumberland County, Pennsylvania, as a free man with no property.

EARLY FERRY AND TAVERN (1787–1802)

1787 January 23rd, John Clark bought the 215 acres known as "Silver Spring" from Samuel Goudy and his wife, Sarah.

• July 13th, the Confederation Congress passed the Northwest Ordinance opening the Northwest Territory.

1788 John Clark and his eldest son, Daniel, settled on Silver Spring's 215 acres and started Clark's Ferry.

1790 The first stone part of the tavern was built around this time. Daniel Clark was recommended for Clark's Tavern's first tavern license.

1792 Christian Miller laid out the nearby community of Petersburg.

1793   A Rye Township Road Petition stated that Daniel "has for some years past established a ferry on the Susquehanna" and "provides for the accommodation of travelers…"

1794   John Clark (the family's patriarch) died of unknown causes.

- The Philadelphia to Lancaster Turnpike was completed.

1795–1798   Daniel Clark was recommended for tavern licenses for Clark's Tavern.

1798   The first description of Clark's "wood and stone" Tavern was made in the U.S. Direct Tax ("Glass Tax").

1799   Robert Clark taxed for property and one ferry in Upper Paxton Township, Dauphin County, and recommended for a tavern license in Cumberland County.

1800   Septennial Census lists Daniel Clark as Ferryman, John Clark (the younger) as Capt. and Robert Clark as Surveyor.

- April 8th, Robert Clark administered John Clark's estate.
- June 20th, Francis Ellis posted a notice of complaint in Harrisburg's *Oracle of Dauphin*.
- July 1st, Daniel Clark responded to Francis Ellis with his own notice in the *Oracle of Dauphin*.
- July 12th, Mathias Flam responded to Daniel Clark with a notice in the *Oracle of Dauphin*.
- September 17th, Daniel Clark died of an unknown illness.
- December 4th, Robert Clark administered his oldest brother, Daniel Clark's estate.

1801   In Cumberland County, Robert Clark was recommended for and received a tavern license for his "house of entertainment."

- July 22nd, in Halifax Township, Dauphin County, the title for Flam's Landing (formerly Huling's Landing) was transferred from Mathias Flam to Robert Clark. Robert bought the property in installments from 1801 until 1804.

PEAK FERRIES AND TAVERN (1802–1837)

1802   Robert Clark and his elder brother, John, were taxed in Rye Township, Cumberland County for 215 acres, 2 horses, 2 cows, and 1 ferry.

- On August 22nd, Robert Clark's elder brother, John, died of unknown causes.
- It is likely Margaret Clark, the matriarch of the family, died this year as well. Robert applied for and received guardianship of the family's youngest children, Ann, Jane, and Peter.
- Robert Clark petitioned Cumberland County's Court to partition, without injury, John Clark's 215 acres in Rye Township equally among John's seven living children. When the court said this could not be done without injuring the property, Robert bought the property in installments from his five siblings. This included the tavern and ferry.

1804   June 6, Robert completed a survey map of a road that went from Brightfield Run to Mary Clark's Ferry.

- June 15, Robert's sister Nancy (Ann) was married at Clark's Tavern to William Ramsey, Deputy-surveyor of Cumberland County.
- November 5th, Robert Clark took ownership of Flam's Landing (50 acres) after making a final payment to Mathias Flam.

1805   In Rye Township, Cumberland County, Robert Clark was taxed for 2 horses, 11 cattle, 1 ferry and 215 acres.

1805–1807   Likely period when Robert Clark built the second stone addition, third stage of the tavern.

1807   Robert Clark was taxed in Halifax Township, Dauphin County, for 50 acres and 1 ferry.

- March 4th, an act to build a turnpike from Harrisburg through Lewistown and Huntingdon to Pittsburgh, was passed by the Commonwealth of Pennsylvania.

1808   Clark's Tavern became a stagecoach stop when Robert became a partner in a newly formed Juniata Mail Stage Company.

- Robert Clark was taxed in Halifax Township, Dauphin County for 1 cow, 1 ferry, and 100 acres.
- Robert Clark was taxed in Rye Township, Cumberland County for 215 acres, 2 horses, 4 cows, and 1 ferry.

1809   Robert Clark ordered "wine and spirits" for Clark's Tavern from John Foster in Harrisburg.

1810   Robert Clark, John Boden, and William Ramsey hired John
        Chisholm from Inverness, Scotland, to build a gristmill.

1811   By April, Robert Clark was appointed Deputy Constable for
        Rye Township, Cumberland County.

- November 28th, Robert's sister, Jane, was married by Rev.
  Mr. Brady at Clark's Tavern to John Boden, High Sheriff of
  Cumberland County.

- Robert was taxed in Rye Township, Cumberland County for
  215 acres and 50 acres, 1 ferry, 1 sawmill, 2 horses, 4 cows, and
  1 lot in Petersburg.

- In Halifax Township, Dauphin County, Robert was taxed for
  150 acres and a ferry.

1812   March 11th, Robert Clark completed a draft of a road
        that began at the Great Road that led from Harrisburg to
        Huntingdon and intersected the Great Road from Clark's Ferry
        to Sherman's Valley.

1814   April, Benjamin Long and his family crossed the Susquehanna
        River from Dauphin County on two of Clark's ferries.

- April 5, Robert became a Deputy Surveyor for Cumberland
  County.

- In Fairfax Township, Dauphin County, Robert Clark was taxed
  for 150 acres, 2 houses, 2 mares, 4 cattle, and 1 ferry.

- In Rye Township, Cumberland County, Robert Clark was taxed
  for four tracts of land consisting of 215, 50, 150, and 53 acres.
  He was also taxed for 1 gristmill and 1 sawmill, 1 ferry, and 2
  lots in Petersburg.

- In Rye Township, Cumberland County, with Boden and Ramsey,
  Robert Clark was taxed for 50 acres and 1 grist mill and sawmill.

- June, in Halifax Township, Dauphin County, Robert Clark
  warranted three tracts of land consisting of 108 acres, 54 acres,
  and 80 perches. and 10 acres 90 perches.

- From August 7, 1814, to February 17, 1815, Robert Clark
  served during the War of 1812 as a 2nd sergeant in Company
  C, 2nd Regiment, the Pennsylvania Militia. In 1814, in

Robert's absence, Joseph Robison was issued a license by Cumberland County to run Clarks Tavern.

- December 27th, Robert filed in Cumberland County's Court, a preliminary "Draft of a Road from Sheep Island in Rye Township to Clark's Ferry."
- May 28th, Robert filed in Cumberland County's Court, a finished "Draft of a Road from Sheep Island in Rye Township to Clark's Ferry."

1817 In Rye Township, Cumberland County, Robert Clark was taxed for four tracks of land; 210, 250, 70, and 50 acres. He was also taxed for a grist mill, a sawmill, and 1 ferry across the Susquehanna River and 1 ferry across Sherman's Creek.

- With John Boden and William Ramsey, Robert Clark was taxed for 50 acres, 1 grist mill, and 1 sawmill.

1818 The Pennsylvania Legislature voted to build a canal bridge across the Susquehanna River at John Clark's Ferry, Later called Robert Clark's Lower Ferry.

- May 8th, John Boden, placed a notice in the *Carlisle Gazette* advertising a committee meeting on June 3rd to discuss possible locations for Clark's Ferry Canal Bridge.
- October 14th, Robert completed a survey map of a road from Thomas Hulings' Ferry on the Juniata River to the public road leading up the Juniata River.

1819 March 26th and 27th, Robert completed a survey map of a road from Clark's Ferry to a point on the Juniata River across from Sheep Island.

1820 March 22nd, an act of the state legislature created Perry County out of the northern part of Cumberland County.

- July 12th, Robert began a new mail stage route from Harrisburg to Bellefonte.
- December 16, Robert Clark was appointed Justice of the Peace for Rye Township.
- In Rye Township, Robert Clark, Boden, and Ramsey were taxed for 266 acres, a grist mill, and a sawmill.

- Robert was taxed in Rye Township, Cumberland County, for two ferries, one across the Susquehanna River and the other across Sherman's Creek and 655 acres.

1822 April 11th, Robert began another mail stage, one between Clark's Ferry and Concord in Franklin County.

- July 25th, the *Perry Forester* announced Robert was a member of the Democratic-Republican Committee.
- October 23rd, Robert announced an expansion of his Bellefonte stage route from Bellefonte to Meadville.

1824 March 27th, the state legislature passed an act that empowered Governor John A. Shulze to appoint three canal commissioners. These commissioners were to determine the best locations for the Pennsylvania Canal.

- Robert gave to Cumberland County Court, a description (viewing) of a proposed road from the Great Northern Turnpike near the mouth of the Juniata River to near New Berry's Falls.
- December 23rd, Robert Clark, along with John Cox of Franklin County and John Harper of Cumberland County, was authorized by the state to survey the boundary line between Cumberland and Perry Counties.
- In Halifax Township, Dauphin County, Robert Clark was taxed for 50 acres, 1 island of 4 acres and *2 ferries*. This is the first record found that stated Robert Clark had two ferries running from Dauphin County.

1825 March 23rd, Robert advertised the start of another new stage line beginning at Clark's Ferry and going through New Bloomfield, Ickesburg, and Landisburg to Douglas' Mill in Blain.

- April 11th, the state legislature added two more canal commissioners, making a total of five. The five commissioners were to hire surveyors and other personnel to determine the costs of building canals at different locations.
- April 25th, an advertisement in the *Oracle of Dauphin* announced fare reductions for Robert Clark and John Blair & Company's stage line from Harrisburg to Pittsburgh.

1826 February 25, a third act of the Pennsylvania State Legislature allowed the canal commissioners to start the construction of the canals.

1827 February 5th, the canal commissioners and Governor Shulze approved an extension of the Eastern Division of the canal to Foster's Falls, just below Robert Clark's Lower Ferry Landing in Dauphin County.

- August 2nd, engineers gave the commissioners estimates for building both tow-path and aqueduct bridges across the Susquehanna River at both Robert Clark's Lower and his Upper Ferry Landings.

- August 3rd, the Canal Board decided, because of lower costs, to extend the Eastern Division of the canal up the Susquehanna River from Foster's Falls to Robert Clark's Upper Ferry Landing, across from the lower end of Duncan's Island.

- August 6th, Charles Mowry, the Acting Canal Commissioner, had handbills printed announcing a meeting for contractors at Baskin's Tavern located at Robert Clark's Upper Ferry Landing.

- August 11th, at the Baskin's Tavern meeting, Robert Clark gave Canal Commissioner Mowry a notice and placed one on the bar-room wall. The notice warned that Robert would prosecute anyone erecting a dam or dams injurious to his ferries or his properties bordering the Susquehanna River. Charles Mowery then awarded dam and canal contract proposals.

- September 10th, on behalf of Robert Clark and the people of Perry County, J. Miller of Philadelphia, gave a presentation to the canal commissioners to convince them to change their minds about the location of the canal bridge. The presentation was unsuccessful.

- In Halifax Township, Dauphin County, Robert Clark was taxed for 300 acres, 2 stone houses (tavern buildings), and 2 ferries.

- November 27th, Robert advertised for rent in the *Oracle of Dauphin,* his Lower Ferry Tavern on the Dauphin County side of the Susquehanna and Clark's Tavern, and several other of his properties on the Perry County side of the river.

1828 Robert Clark was taxed in Halifax Township, Dauphin County for 3 stone houses and 2 wooden houses and 2 ferries. Cornelius Baskins was taxed $150 for keeping a tavern in Robert Clark's upper ferry tavern building.

- The covered tow-path canal bridge across the Susquehanna River from Clark's Upper Ferry Landing to the southern point of Duncan's small island was almost completed when ice floods set back its opening.

1829 Robert Clark was one of five commissioners who supervised the building of the state road that went from the west end of the Harrisburg Bridge to Petersburg.

1830 March 19th, Robert Clark petitioned the Commonwealth's Canal Commission for $43,600 in compensation for the destruction of his property and ferry businesses in building the canal. The canal commission refused to accept responsibility for most of his losses and recommended Robert be paid $500 in compensation.

- September 25th, the Canal Board reconsidered Robert Clark's request for compensation and decided to offer him $1,000.
- December 31st, a Board of Appraisers determined Robert Clark should be given $2,100 in compensation for his loses and the canal commission approved.

1831 Cornelius Baskins was taxed for leasing Clark's tavern building at his Upper Ferry Landing and Jacob Fester for leasing Robert's tavern building at what had been his Lower Ferry Landing.

- The Commonwealth of Pennsylvania was still working on making Clark's Ferry Bridge safe to use.

1832 November 15, the Superintendent of the Eastern Division of the Canal reported that the "Clark's Ferry bridge has undergone a thorough repair, the original defects in that structure have been remedied" and the bridge was declared safe to use.

- June 29th, Robert Clark sold three tracts of land in Halifax Township, Dauphin County, to Jacob M. Haldeman and Thomas Elder for $1,000.

1833   Cornelius Baskins leased Clark's tavern building at his Upper Ferry Landing, and Jacob Fester leased Robert's tavern building at what had been his Lower Ferry Lending.

1834   James Freeland leased the tavern building at Robert Clark's Upper Ferry Landing while John Martin leased Robert Clark's tavern building at his former Lower Ferry Landing.

- Robert Clark was taxed in Halifax Township Dauphin County for two stone houses and 4 log/frame houses.

1835   James Freeland still leased the tavern building at Robert Clark's Upper Ferry Landing while John Martin still leased Robert's tavern building at the former Lower Ferry Landing.

- November 17th , Presbyterian minister, Matthew Patterson, married Robert Clark to Margaretta Bovard at Clark's Ferry Tavern.

1836   June 22nd & 23rd, Robert Clark and his wife Margaretta sold Robert's last 2 tracts of land in Dauphin County, to Jacob Haldeman. These sales included the former location of Clark's Lower Ferry Landing, his Upper Ferry Landing, and his ferry rights. This officially ended Clark's ferries across the Susquehanna River.

- Robert and Margaretta's only daughter, Christina, was born.

POST-FERRY (1837–1875)

1837   Robert and Margaretta Clark's only son, John, was born.

- In Halifax Township, Dauphin County, Benjamin Richard ran Haldeman's Tavern at Robert Clark's former Upper Ferry Landing, and the Widow Freeland ran Haldeman's Tavern at Clark's former Lower Ferry Landing.

1840   The 1840 Census showed Robert and Margaretta Clark living with their family at Clark's Tavern.

1842   October 10th, sick with fever and chills, Robert Clark dictated his Last Will and Testament at Clark's Tavern but recovered from his illness.

1850 The Census showed Robert Clark (age 70) and his wife, Margaretta Clark (age 33), living with their extended family at the farm Margaretta inherited from her father in Saville Township.

1855 April 15th, Robert Clark died, and his wife, Margaretta, inherited Silver Spring's 215 acres as well as Clark's tavern building.

1862 Duncannon oral tradition has it that part of Company B, of the Thirteenth Pennsylvania Reserves (the famed Pennsylvania Regiment), mustered at the Clark's tavern building.

1865 March 17th, 18th, and 19th, a devastating Susquehanna River flood swept away all the structures at Clark's tavern except the stone tavern building, which it left in ruins.

1869 April 10th, Margaretta and her second husband, Zachariah Rice, sold 200 acres of "Silver Spring" (including Clark's Tavern building) to William King, Joseph Swartz, and John Shively.

1874 February 18th, Margaretta (Clark) Rice died.

POST-TAVERN (1875–PRESENT)

1875 King, Shively, and Swartz sold the ruined tavern building and adjoining two lots to two brothers, David and Enos Smith.

1875–1880 David and Enos remodeled the tavern's original two stone sections into three apartments. In the former location of Goudy's original log house, they built an attached balloon-framed structure to be used as a fourth apartment.

1880 April 4th, the tavern building and adjoining lots were sold at a sheriff's sale to Enos and Michael Smith, who used the tavern building as three apartments. The Smith's combined the two apartments on the North Market Street side into one for their personal use.

1880–1974 Starting with Enos Smith, three generations of Smiths lived in the front (North Market Street) apartment for 94 years and rented the other two.

1974 Max Smith sold the tavern building to Isabel Kunkel and Janet Leins to use as a private dwelling.

1974–2012 The tavern building was used as a private dwelling and apartments, but over time became unlivable because of neglect and vandalism.

2012 The Borough of Duncannon bought the abandoned and deteriorated tavern building and two adjoining lots to save the building from demolition.

2015 December 22nd, the Borough of Duncannon transferred the ownership of the Clark's Tavern and its two adjoining lots to the Historical Society of Perry County for preservation and future restoration.

NOTES

PART I: A HISTORY OF CLARK'S FERRIES AND TAVERNS

1. Theodore K. Long, *Forty Letters to Carson Long* (New Bloomfield: Carson Long, 1931) 12–13.

2. Francis Ellis and Austin Hungerford, *History of that Part of the Susquehanna and Juniata Valleys Embraced in the Counties of Mifflin, Juniata, Perry, Union and Snyder, In the Commonwealth of Pennsylvania,* vol. 1–2 (Philadelphia: Everts, Peck & Richards, 1886).

CHAPTER 1: PRE-FERRY AND TAVERN TIME PERIOD (1766–1787)

1. "Marcus Hulings's Survey," 1769, Pennsylvania State Archives, www.phmc.pa .gov/Archives Research-Online/Pages/Land-Records-Overview.aspx (accessed March 21, 2017).

2. Samuel Goudy, "To Be Sold" advertisement, *Carlisle Gazette,* 27 December 1785.Here after cited Goudy, *advertisement.*

3. Cumberland County Commissioners' Office, Tax Rates Books, 1786, Rye Township, microfilm roll 150, Cumberland County Historical Society (Carlisle, PA).

4. Goudy, *advertisement.*

5. Ibid.

CHAPTER 2: EARLY FERRY AND TAVERN TIME PERIOD (1787–1802)

1. Victor Hart and Jason Wilson, "Clark's Ferry and Tavern," Special Issue: *The Juniata Valley, Pennsylvania History: A Journal of Mid-Atlantic,* v. 83, no. 2, (Spring, 2016), 140.

2. Cumberland County Recorder of Deeds, Title Transfer, 1787, Samuel Goudy and his wife to John Clark, record book, vol. 1, book H, p. 384, Cumberland County Recorder of Deeds Cumberland County Historical Society (Carlisle, PA).

3. Perry County Recorder of Deeds, Title Transfer, 1875, Margaretta and Zachariah Rice to King, Swartz and Shively, *Deed Index,* FamilySearch, https:familysearch.org (accessed May 3, 2017).

4. Cumberland County Commissioners, Tax Rates Books, 1787, Rye Township, microfilm roll 150, Cumberland County Historical Society (Carlisle, PA).

5. Cumberland County Prothonotary, 1798, Naturalization Appearance Docket. Case #156, August, Cumberland County Archives (Carlisle, PA).

6. Ibid.

7. U.S. Department of the Interior, *Decennial Census*, 1850, Perry County, series M432, microfilm roll 805, Cumberland County Historical Society (Carlisle, PA).

8. Ohio History Central, "Northwest Territory," 2015, www.ohiohistorycentral .org/w/North,west_Territory?rec=772 (assessed March 15, 2016).

9. Ms. Terry Stewart,"The Highland Clearances," *Historic UK.* 2017, www .historic-uk.com/HistoryUK/History of Scotland/ (assessed August 10, 2017).

10. "Married Friday last at Clark's Ferry." *Kline's Gazette,* 20 June 1804.

11. "Married last evening at Robert Clark's." *Kline's Gazette*, 29 November 1811.

12. Ellis, vol. 1.

13. George Way, *Scottish Clan & Family Encyclopedia* (Glasgow: HarperCollins, 1994.)

14. William Henry Egle, ed., *Notes and Queries: Historical, Biographical and Genealogical:Chiefly Relating to Interior Pennsylvania,* vol. 1. (Harrrisburg: *Daily Telegraph*, 1887), 389.

15. Luther Reily Kelker, *History of Dauphin County Pennsylvania,* vol. 1. (New York : Lewis Publishing Company, 1907). 435.

16. Egle, 390.

17. Mathias Flam, "To the Public," *Oracle of Dauphin*, Harrisburg, vol. VIII. no. XXXVII, 12 July 1800.

18. John Agnew, "Order to view a road from Hackets to Sandersons," 8 August 1788, Lenig Library, Perry Historians (New Bloomfield, PA).

19. *Wright's to Juniata Map*, May 11, 1820, Map #1892, A15, Cabinet 7, Drawer D1, Pennsylvania State Archives (Harrisburg, PA).

20. Dauphin County Recorder of Deeds, Title Transfer, 15 October 1785, Marcus Huling to Thomas Huling, FamilySearch, www.family search.com. (accessed 16 February 201).

21. George Shumway, et al. *Conestoga Wagon 1750–1850: Freight Carrier for 100 Years of Americas Westward Expansion* (York: Early American Indistries Association, 1964) 61–64.

22. Ibid.

23. Ken Frew, telephone conversation with author, July 15, 2017.

24. George Shumway, 61.

25. Norman Wilkinson and George Beyer, *The Conestoga Wagon,* Leaflet No. 5 (Harrisburg: Pennsylvania Historical and Museum Commission, 1997).

26. Ibid.

27. Ibid.

28. Joseph Jefferies and John Wright, "To Our Friends," 7 December 1787, *Pennsylvania Chronicle* in George Reeser Prowell, "River Ferries Over the Susquehanna—Wrights and Anderson" (Lancaster: Lancaster Historical Society, 1923).

29. Goudy, *advertisement.*

30. Max Smith, telephone communication with author, February 19, 2015.

31. J. Randall Cotton, "Log Houses in America," *Old-House Journal,* January/February, 1990, 37–44.

32. Kim S. Rice, *Early American Taverns: For the Entertainment of Friends and Strangers* (Chicago:Regnery Gateway, 1983), 20.

33. Grace Winthrop, "Early Inns and Taverns." *History Quartlt Digital Archives,* 1987, www.tehistory.org (accessed February 2, 2017).

34. Cumberland County Clerk of Courts, Tavern License Application, 1790, Daniel Clark. RG/024/2T, boxes 1 and 2, Pennsylvania State Archives (Harrisburg, PA).

35. Rice, 64–65.

36. Daniel Clark, Road Petition, 1793, Cumberland County Quarter Sessions Docket #7, pp. 120, 130 and 142, Cumberland County Archives (Cumberland County, PA)

37. Cumberland County Clerk of Courts, Tavern License Application, 1794, Daniel Clark, RG/024/2T, boxes 1 and 2, Pennsylvania State Archives (Harrisburg, PA).

38. Cumberland County Clerk of Court, Tavern License Recommendation, 1799, Daniel Clark

39. Ed Crews,"Drinking in Colonial America," 2017, History.org. www. history .org/foundation/journal/ holiday07/drink.cfm (accessed September 13, 2017).

40. Samuel Goudy, 1785.

41. Cumberland County Orphans' Court, John Clark's Estate Inventory, 1800, microfilm roll C-039, Cumberland County Historical Society (Carlisle, PA).

42. Rice, 96

43. "History of Spirits in America,*"* Distilled Spirits Council of the United States, 2017, www.discus.or/heritage/spirits/#2 (accessed March 20, 2017).

44. John Clark's Estate Inventory, 1800.

45. *History of Scotch Whisky.* Scotch Whiskey Association, 2012, www.scotch whisky.org.uk/understanding-scotch/history-of-whisky/ (accessed April 30, 2017).

46. John Clark's Estate Inventory, 1800.

47. Bill Toland, "Rye is Popular Again," *Post Gazett.* May 23, 2007, www.post gazetter.com/libations /2007/05/23/Rye (accessed April 30, 2017).

48. Cutty, "Grain Volumes for Whiskey and Vodka," 2011, adiforums.com (accessed June 28, 2017).

49. Cumberland County Commissioners, Tax Rates Books, 1786, Rye Township, microfilm roll 151.

50. Dauphin County Recorder of Deeds, Title Transfer, 1804, Mathias Flam to Robert Clark, microfilmroll #1510, Pennsylvania State Archives (Harrisburg, PA).

51. Hain, 265

52. *Recipies from Scotland; 1680s to 1940s,* National Library of Scotland, 201, digital.nis.uk/recipes/themes/index.html (Accessed July 4, 2017).

53. "George Washinton's Infamous Small Beer Recipe." American Homebrewers Association, 2017, https://www.homebrewerassociation.org/how-to-brew/george-wash ingtons infamous small-beer-recipe (Accessed July 4, 2017).

54. "History of Spirits in America"

55. Cumberland County Tavern License Petitions, Rye Township, 1790–1808, RG/025/2T, boxes 1–2, Pennsylvania State Archives, Harrisburg, PA.

56. Cumberland County Commissioners, Tavern Records and Licenses, 1750–1855, CCPA Archives, https://ccweb.ccpa.net/archives/RecordGroups.

57. Ibid.

58. Ellis, 1058; Hain, 954.

59. Cumberland County Tavern License Petitions, Rye Township, 1819–1820, Cumberland County Archives Listings: Record Groups, https://ccweb.ccpa.net/archives/RecordGroups (accessed June 3, 2018).

60. Hain, 953.

61. Robert Clark, "Valuable Property for Rent," 1827.

62. Perry County Commissioners, Tax Rate Books 1829–1830, Wheatfield Township, FamilySearch, https://www. familysearch.org/search/catalog (accessed March 27, 2019).

63. Silas B. Wright, History of Perry County: From the Earliest Settlement to the Present Time (Harvard: Wylie & Griest, 1873), 40.

64. Perry County Commissioners, Tax Rate Books, 1842, Penn Township, Lenig Library, Perry Historians, New Bloomfield, PA

65. Perry County Commissioners, Tax Rate Books, 1844, 1845, 1847, 1849 and 1850, Penn Township.

66. Perry County Commissioners, Tax Rate Books, 1853, Penn Township.

67. Perry County Commissioners, Tax Rate Books 1842, 1844, 1845, 1847, 1850, and 1853, Petersburg.

68. John Lewis Kremmel, *Interior of an American Inn,* 1813, Toledo Museum of Art

69. John Clark's Estate Inventory, 1800.

70. Rice, 85.

71. Henky Gray Graham. *The Social Life of Scotland in the Eighteenth Century.* (London: Adam and Charles Black, 1901).

72. Cumberland County Commissioners, Tax Rates Books, 1788, Rye Township, microfilm roll 151, Cumberland County Historical Society (Carlisle, PA).

73. Cumberland County Commissioners, Tax Rates Books, 1789, Rye Township, microfilm roll 151, Cumberland County Historical Society (Carlisle, PA)

74. Graham, *The Social Life of Scotland,* 58.

75. Ibid., 175.

76. Ibid., 179

77. "A Social History of Scotland," *Category Archives: 17th and 18th Centuries,* n.d., www.nickloggie.com/category/17th-and-18th-centuries/ (April 10, 2017).

78. Graham, 59.

79. *Recipies from Scotland; 1680s to 1940s.*

80. "Oatmeal Bannock," *A Bread A Day,* 2009, www.abreadaday.com/oameal-bannock/ (accessed August 20, 2017).

81. "A Social History of Scotland."

82. Graham, 181.

83. Hain, 156.

84. Graham, 510.

85. John Clark's Estate Inventory, 1800.

86. Graham, 179.

87. Mrs. Frazer, *The Practice of Cookery, Pastry, Pickling, Rreserving, & ....* (Edinburgh: PeterHill, 1791)

88. *Recipies from Scotland; 1680's to 1940's.*

89. Mrs. Frazer, 63

90. Thomas Somerville, *My Own Life and Times, 1741–1830.* (Edinburgh : Edmonston & Douglas, 1861) 335.

91. Mrs. Frazer, 3.

92. Mrs. Frazer, 1–3

93. Ellis, 1061.

94. Hart and Wilson, 2016.

95. John Clark's Estate Inventory, 1800.

96. United States Federal Government, *U.S. Direct Tax,* 1798, Cumberland County, PA, Rye Township (Washington , D.C).

97. Hain, 389.

98. Ibid., 395.

99. *U.S. Direct Tax,* 1798.

100. Rice 78–83

101. Kelker, 410

102. Rice, 83.

103. Rice, 102.

104. John Clark's Estate Inventory, 1800.

105. *U.S. Direct Tax,* 1798.

106. Rice,103–104.

107. Petition to Award an Inquest, 1802

108. Hain, 285.

109. Ibid, 298.

110. Ibid, 295–296.

111. Cumberland County Tavern License Recommendation, 1790.

112. Cumberland County Tavern License Recommendation, 1794.

113. Cumberland County Orphans' Court, Robert Clark Appointed Guardian of Jane, Nancy (Ann) and Peter Clark 1802, microfilm roll 1, vol. 1–3 p.366, Cumberland County Historical Society (Carlisle, PA).

114. *U.S. Direct Ta ,* 1798.

115. Cumberland County Tax Rates Books, 1797, 1798, 1799.

116. "Died on Wednesday Last," *Oracle of Dauphin*, 1800, September 22: 3.

117. Letter from Mrs. Harry Boden Fairthorne IV. to Mrs. Janet Kliens, October 6, 1975. Boden folder. Cumberland County Historical Society (Carlisle, PA)

118. John Clark's Estate Inventory, 1800.

119. "1800 - Died on Wednesday last," *Oracle of Dauphin.*

120. "Daniel Clark died on Wednesday last at the mouth of the Juniata," *Kline's Gazette.* 24 September 1800.

121. Suzanne M. Shultz, "Epidemics in Colonial Americafrom 1699–1799 and the Risk of Dyng." *Archiving Early America.* 2007–2017. www.varsitytutors.com/early america/earlyamerica.../early-american-epidemics (accessed March 8, 2017).

122. William Pencak, "The Promise of Rvolutions: 1750–1800," *Pennsylvania: A History of the Commonwealth*, ed. Randall M.: Pencak, Miller (University Park: Pennsylvania University Press, 2000) 105–152.

123. *U.S. Direct Tax,* 1798.

124. Hart and Wilson, 2016.

125. John Clark's Estate Inventory, 1800.

126. Letter from Mrs. Harry Boden Fairthorne IV., 1975.

127. Daniel Clark's Estate Inventory, 6 March 1801, microfilm # C098, Cumberland County Historical Society (Carlisle, PA).

128. Mathias Flam, "To the Public," *Oracle of Delphi,* 12 July 1800, vol. VIII, no. XXXVII.

129. Dauphin County Tax Rates Books, 1800, Upper Paxton Township, microfilm roll 4141, Pennsylvania State Archives (Harrisburg, PA).

CHAPTER 3: PEAK FERRY AND TAVERN TIME PERIOD (1802–1836)

1. Mathias Flam, 12 July 1800.

2. Dauphin County Recorder of Deeds, Title Transfer, 1804, Mathias Flam to Robert Clark, microfilm roll 1510, Pennsylvania State Archives (Harrisburg, PA).

3. Cumberland County License Recommendation, 1801.

4. Cumberland County Orphans' Court, 10 October 1802, Robert Clark
Appointed Guardian of Jane, Nancy (Ann) and Peter Clark, *Pennsylvania ProbateRecord, 1683–1794*, vol. 1–3 p. 366, Cumberland County Historical Society (Carlisle, PA).

5. Cumberland County Orphans' Court, 1802. Robert Clark's Petition to Award and Inquest to Partition John Clark's 215 Acres of Land Among John's Seven Children. microfilm roll 1, vol. 1–3, pages 358–359, Cumberland County Historical Society (Carlisle,PA).

6. "Mortuary Notice," 30 August 1802, *Oracle of Dauphin* (Harrisburg, PA).

7. Pennsylvania Septennial Census Records, 1800, Box 1026, microfilm, 14 rolls. Records of the House of Representatives. Records of the General Assembly, Record Group 7. Pennsylvania Historical and Museum Commission, Harrisburg, PA.

8. Robert Clark, "Letter from Robert Clark to James Hamilton," 11 September, 1802. Hamilton Papers. Cumberland County Historical Society (Carlisle, PA).

9. Cumberland County Orphans' Court, Request for the Court to Confirm John Clark's Estate to Robert Clark, 10 October, 1802, microfilm roll 1, Vol. 1–3. p. 366–368, Cumberland County Historical Society (Carlisle, PA).

10. Ibid.

11. Pennsylvania Septennial Census Records, 1800, Box 1026, microfilm, 14 rolls. Records of the House of Representatives. Records of the General Assembly, Record Group 7. Pennsylvania Historical and Museum Commission, Harrisburg, PA.

12. U.S. Department of the Interior, 1850, Perry County, PA, Saville Township, microfilm roll 805, Cumberland County Historical Society (Carlisle, PA).

13. Donald C. Jackson, "Roads Most Traveled; Turnpikes in Southeastern Pennsylvania in the Early Republic". Ed. Judith McGaw, *Early American Technology: Making and Doing Things From the Colonial Era to 1850* (UNC Press Books, 2014) 197–239.

14. Commonwealth of Pennsylvania, "Historic Context for Transportation Networks in Pennsylvania," 8–9, www.dot7.state.pa.us/CRGIS_Attachments/Survey /Transportation Networks_Historic_Context.pdf (accessed October 15, 2017).

15. Cumberland County Orphans' Court, Request for the Court to Confirm John Clark's Estate to Robert Clark, 10 October, 1802.

16. U.S. Department of the Interior, *Decennial Census*, 1810, Cumberland County, Rye Township, *FamilySearch*, https:/www.familysearch.org/search/catalog/results? Cou nt=20&placeId=337&query=%2Bplace%3A"United States" %2Bsubject%3Acensus %2 Bavaila bility%3AOnline (accessed November 29, 2017).

17. Robert Clark, "Survey Draft and Report of a Road from Brightfields Run to Clark's Ferry," 6 June 1804, map folder, Lenig Library, Perry Historians (New Bloomfield, PA).

18. Robert Clark, "Survey Petition for a Road from the Great Road from Harrisburg to Huntingdon Intersecting the Great Road from Clark's Ferry to Sherman's Valley," 11 March 1812, map folder, Lenig Library, Perry Historians, New Bloomfield, PA.

19. Robert Clark, "Survey Draft of Road from Sheep Island in Rye Township Cumberland County to Clark's Ferry," 27 December 1815, map folder, Lenig Library, Perry Historians (Newport, PA).

20. Robert Clark, "Draft of Road Beginning Along the Juniata River Opposite Sheep Island to Clark's Ferry on the Susquehanna River." 28 May 1816, map folder, Lenig Library, Perry Historians (New Bloomfield, PA).

21. Robert Clark, "Survey Draft of Road from Thomas Huling's Ferry on the Juniata River to the Public Road Leading Up the Juniata River," 14 October 1818, map folder Lenig Library, Perry Historians (New Bloomfield, PA).

22. Robert Clark, "Survey Draft of Road from Clark's Ferry House to a Point Across from Sheep Island on the Juniata River," 26 & 27 March 1819, map folder, Lenig Library, Perry Historians (New Bloomfield, PA).

23. Robert Clark, "Road Viewing for a Proposed Road from the Great Northern Turnpike Road Near the Mouth of the Juniata River to New Berry's Falls, 13 April 1824, map folder, Lenig Library, Perry Historians (New Bloomfield, PA.

24. Hain, 210.

25. Ellis, 428–429.

26. Hain, 363.

27. Ellis,1070.

28. Letter from Robert Clark to John Foster, 1808, Foster Collection, Dauphin County Historical Society (Harrisburg, PA).

29. Hain, 366.

30. Ibid., 367.

31. Ibid.

32. Ibid.

33. Robert Clark, John Blair and Co., "Stage fare reduced on the Northern Route turnpike road from Harrisburg to Pittsburg," *Oracle of Dauphin*, Vol. 24, No. 30, 23 April 1825.

34. Hain, 368.

35. Ibid.

36. Ellis, 1076.

37. Hain, , 953.

38. Cumberland County Commissioners, Tax Rates Books, 1814, Rye Township, FamilySearch, https://www.familysearch.org/search/catalog (accessed July 18, 2018).

39. Cumberland County Commissioners, Tax Rates Rooks, 1817, Rye Township, FamilySearch, https://www. familysearch.org/search/catalog (accessed July 18, 2018).

40. Ellis, 1075

41. Ibid., 1069

42. John Boden, "Clark's Ferry Bridge," *Carlisle Gazette,* 1818.

43. Dauphin County Commissioners, Tax Rates Books, 1824, Halifax Township, FamilySearch, https://www.familysearch.org/search/catalog (accessed June 29, 2018).

44. Ibid.

45. "Draught of Turnpike from Harrisburg Bridge to Millerstown," June 1822, (T-23) A (9) VII 5574 77, Pennsylvania State Archives (Harrisburg, PA).

46. Dauphin County Commisioners. Tax Rates Books, 1827, Fairfax Township, FamilySearch. https://www.familysearch.org/search/catalog (accessed June 29, 2018).

47. Ibid.

48. *Map Book 1810–1881,* Canal Commissioners, RG-17, Series 452, PHMC, http://www.phmc.state.pa.us/bah/dam/rg/di/r017_0452_CanalMapBooks/Canal Maps Interface.htm (accessed February 7, 2018).

49. Ibid.

50. William H. Shank, *The Amazing Pennsylvania Canals* (York: American Canal and Transportation Center, 1981) 26, 49.

51. *Map Book 1810–1881,* Board of Canal Commissioners.

52. "The Six Clark Ferry Bridges," *American Canals,* 1983, No. 44.

53. Shank, *The Amazing Pennsylvania Canal.*

54. Masters, 31.

55. Ibid., 38–39.

56. Ibid.

57. Ibid., 47.

58. Ibid., 58.

59. Ibid., 60.

60. Ibid., 59

61. Ibid.

62. Ibid., 60.

63. Ibid.

64. Ibid., 40–42.

65. Ibid., 62, 25.

66. Ibid., 28.

67. Ibid.

68. "The Six Clark Ferry Bridges."

69. Masters.

70. Ibid.

71. Ibid.

72. Ibid., 77.

73. Ibid., 83.

74. Ibid., 84.

75. Ibid., 98.

76. Ibid., 109.

77. Ibid., 114.

78. "The Six Clark Ferry Bridges."

79. Ibid.

80. Dauphin County Commissioners, Tax Rates Books, 1832, Halifax Township, FamilySearch, https://www.familysearch.org/search/catalog (accessed June 29, 2018)

81. *Harrisburg Chronicle*, 1833

82. Dauphin County Commissioners, Tax Rates Books, 1833, Halifax Township, FamilySearch, https://www.familysearch.org/search/catalog (accessed June 29, 2018).

83. Dauphin CountyCommissioners, Tax Rates Books, 1834, Halifax Township, Family*Search,* https://www.familysearch.org/search/catalog (accessed June 29, 2018).

84. Dauphin County Commissioners, Tax Rates Books, 1835, Halifax Township, FamilySearch, https://www.familysearch.org/search/catalog (accessed June 29, 2018).

85. Dauphin County Recorder of Deeds, Title Transfer, 1836, Robert Clark and Wife, Maragareta toJacob Haldman, July and August, Book I, vol. 2, pp. 134–139. FamilySearch, https:// www. familysearch.org/search/catalog (accessed February 4, 2019).

86. Dauphin County Commissioners, Tax Rates Books, 1837, Halifax Township, FamilySearch, https:// www.familysearch.org/search/catalog (accessed June 29, 2018).

87. Dauphin County Commissioners, Tax Rates Book, 1828 and 1831, Halifax Township, FamilySearch, https://www.familysearch.org/search/catalog (accessed October 18, 2018).

88. Dauphin County Commissioners, Tax Rates Books, 1836, Halifax Township, FamilySearch, https://www.familysearch.org/search/catalog (accessed June 29, 2018).

89. "Married Friday Last at Clark's Ferry," *Kline's Gazette*, Carlisle, 20 June 1804.

90. Cumberland County Clerk of Courts, Quarter Sessions Dockets, April 1811, #11, pg.278.

91. "Married last evening at Robert Clark's." *Kline's Gazette*, Carlisle, 29 November 1811.

92. Letter from Mrs. Harry Boden Fairthorne IV, 1975.

93. Commonwealth of Pennsylvania, Department of Military Affairs, "Record of Burial Place of Veteran, Perry County," March 22, 1937, (Harrisburg, PA).

94. Cumberland County Clerk of Courts, Tavern License Application, 1814, RG/024/2T, boxes 1 and 2, Pennsylvania State Archives, (Harrisburg, PA).

95. Hain, 317.

96. "Robert Clark, Justice of the Peace" *Perry Forester*, Landisburg, 16 December 1820.

97. "Robert Clark a Member of the Domocratic Republican Committee." *Perry Forester*, Landisburg , 25 July 1822.

98. *Democratic-Republican Party*, American History USA, https://www.american historyusa.com /topic/democratic-republican-party/ (accessed May 2, 2018).

99. Robert Clark, "Valuable Property for Rent," 1827.

100. "Robert Clark married Margaretta," *American Volunteer*, Carlisle, 26 November 1835.

101. Hain, 1045.

102. Letter from Mrs. Harry Boden Fairthorne IV, 1975.

CHAPTER 4: POST-FERRY TIME PERIOD (1836–1875)

1. Ibid.

2. Ibid.

3. "Petition to the Court of Perry County for a Road From Petersburg to the Month of Sherman's Creek," August 11. 1837, Lenig Library, Perry Historians (New Bloomfield, PA).

4. Hain, 1042.

5. U.S. Department of the Interior, *Decennial Census*, 1840, Perry County, PA, Penn Township, National Archives and Records Administration, Series M432, roll 805, Pennsylvania State Archives (Harrisburg, PA).

6. Robert Clark, "Last Will and Testament," 11 August 1842 (filed New Bloomfield Court House, May 16, 1855).

7. Ibid.

8. Hain, 953. Ellis, 1069.

9. Department of Military Affairs, "Record of Burial Place of Veteran.".

10. "Robert Clark's Death," *Perry County Democrat,* 26 April1855.

11. "Died at Clark's Ferry," *Freeman,* 26 April 1855.

12. Robert Clark, "Last Will and Testament."

13. Hart and Wilson, 153.

14. Hain, 389.

15. Old Timer, "The Letter Box," n.d., Lenig Library (Newport, PA).

16. Perry County Recorder of Deeds, 1869.

17. Hain, 953.

CHAPTER 5: POST-TAVERN TIME PERIOD (1836–1875)

1. Perry County Recorder of Deeds, Title Transfer, King, Swartz & Shively to Grantee, David Smith. 1875, Book J, Vol. II, Page 25.

2. Hart and Wilson, 2016.

3. Stephen O. Smith, conversation with author during tavern house inspection, September 3, 2015.

4. Max Smith, email to author, October 22, 2017.

5. Ibid.

6. "Owners of Old Tavern Seek Date," *Duncannon Record,* 16 September 1974.

7. Perry County Recorder of Deeds, Landex2012205944, 30 July 2012, New Bloomfield.

8. Agreement for "Clark's Ferry Tavern" Property, Pennsylvania Commonwealth, Perry County, Duncannon, September 23, 2015.

PART II: A PRELIMINARY STUDY OF THE ARCHITECTUAL FEATURES OF CLARK'S TAVERN, DUNCANNON, PENNSYLVANIA

1. Goudy, *advertisement.*

2. Max Smith, telephone conversation with author, February 19, 2015.

3. U. S. Direct Tax, 1798.

4. Hain, 389.

5. Old Timer, n.d.

6. Perry County Recorder of Deeds, 1875, Title Transfer, King, Swartz & Shively to Grantee, David Smith

7. Perry County, Recorder of Deeds, 1875 and 1880.

8. *Anatomy of a Home,* Inquiring Eye Home Inspections, LLC, www.inquiring-eye .com (accessed February 15, 2019).

9. Ellis, 1061.

10. Cumberland County Tavern License, 1790, RG/024/2T, boxes 1 and 2, Pennsylvania State Archives, (Harrisburg, PA).

11. *U.S. Direct Tax,* 1798.

12. Donald Jackson, 2014.

13. Kim Rice, 1983.

14. Lenig Library, folder 165, Perry Historians (New Bloomfield, PA).

15. Perry County Title Transfer, 1875.

16. Old Timer, n.d.

17. Perry County Title Transfer, 1875.

18. Perry County Title Transfer, 1880.

19. Max Smith, email to author, October 22, 2017.

CHAPTER 7: STAGE 2 – THE FIRST STONE ADDITION, APARTMENT-A

1. Max Smith, February 19, 2015.
2. Thomas Visser, "Nails: Clues to a Building's History," 1997, University of Vermont, Historic Preservation Program, www.uvm.edu/-histpres/203/nails.html (accessed October 30, 2017).
3. James Garvin, James. *A Building History of Northern New England,* (Hanover: University Press of New England, 2001.)
4. Max Smith, February 19, 2015.
5. Steve Smith, November 1, 2014.
6. Max Smith, February 19, 2015.
7. Ibid.
8. Ibid.
9. Ibid.
10. Max Smith, email communication with author, November 3, 2017.
11. Ibid.

CHAPTER 8: STAGE 3 – THE SECOND STONE ADDITION, APARTMENTS B AND C

1. Jackson, 2014.
2. Rice, 1983.
3. U.S. Secretary of State, Decennial Census, 1800.
4. Hain, 389.
5. Max Smith, October 22, 2017.
6. Ibid.
7. Ibid.
8. Max Smith, October 22, 2017.
9. Old Timer, n.d.
10. Max Smith, February 19, 2015.
11. Max Smith, October 22, 2017.

APPENDIX A: SURVEY ROAD MAPS

1. Robert Clark, 6 June 1804.
2. Robert Clark, 11 March 1812.
3. Robert Clark, 27 December 1815.
4. Robert Clark, 28 May 1816.
5. Robert Clark, 14 October 1818.
6. Robert Clark, 26 & 27 March 1819.
7. Robert Clark, 13 April 1824.

BIBLIOGRAPHY

American Canal Society. 1983. "The Six Clark Ferry Bridges." *American Canals* 44. York:American Canal Society.

American History USA. 2012–2018. *Democratic-Republican Party*. https://www .americanhistoryusa.com/topic/democratic-republican-party (accessed May 2, 2018).

American Homebrewers Association. 2017. *George Washinton's Infamous Small Beer Recipe*. https://www.homebrewerassociation.org/how-to-brew/george-washingtons -infamous-small-beer-recipe (accessed July 4, 2017).

American Volunteer. "Robert Clark married Margaretta." November 26, 1835.

"Anatomy of a Home." Inquiring Eye Home Inspections. www.inquiring-eye.com (accessed February 15, 2019).

Baskins et. al., Cornelius. 1837. Petition to the Court of Perry County for a Road From Petersburg to the Mouth of Sherman's Creek. August 11. Lening Library, Perry Historians, Newport, PA

Boden, John. "Clark's Ferry Bridge." *Carlisle Gazette.* 1818.

Boden, Mrs. Harry IV. Letter from Mrs Harry Boden to Mrs. Janet K. Leins. October 6, 1975. Boden File. Cumberland County Historical Society. Carlisle, PA.

"Bread A Day." 2009. Oatmeal Bannock. September 2. https://www.abread aday.com /oameal-bannock/ (accessed August 20, 2017).

Carlisle Herald. "Married Friday at Clark's Ferry." June 20, 1804.

Clark, Daniel. *Oracle of Dauphin.* July 14 & 21, 1800.

Clark, Robert. Letter from Robert Clark to James Hamilton. September 11, 1802. M.S. Hamilton Folder. Cumberland County Archives, Carlisle, PA.

———. 1804. Survey Road Draft and Report of a Road from Brightfields Run to Clark's Ferry. June 6. Cumberland County Clerk of Courts Road & Bridge Papers. Map Folder. Lenig library, Perry Historians, Newport, PA.

———. 1808. Letter from Robert Clark to John Foster. Foster Collection. Dauphin County Historical Society, Harrisburg, PA.

———. 1812. Survey Petition for a Road from the Great Road from Harrisburg to Huntindon Interesecting the Great Road from Clark's Ferry to Sherman's Valley. March 11. Cumberland County Clerk of Courts Road & Bridge Papers. Box 5. Folder 42. Cumberland County Archives, Carlisle, PA.

———. 1815. Survey Road Draft from Sheep Island in Rye Township Cumberland County to Clark's Ferry. December 17. Map Folder. Lenig Library, Perry Historians, Newport, PA.

———. 1816. Survey Road Draft from Sheep Island in Rye Township to Clark's Ferry. May 28. Map Folder. Lenig Library, Perry Historians. Newport, PA.

———. 1818. Survey Road Draft of the Junction of the Public Road Leading up the Juniata River to the road leading to Clark's Mill. October 14. Map File. Lenig Library, Perry Historians, Newport, PA.

———. 1819. Survey Draft of Road from Clark's Ferry to a Point on the Juniata River Across from Sheep Island. March 26 & 27. Map Folder. Lenig Library, Perry Historians, Newport, PA.

———. 1824. Road Viewing for Proposed Road from the Great Northern Turnpike Road Near the Mouth of the Juniata River to Near New Berry's Falls. April 30. Map Folder. Lenig Library, Perry Historians, Newport, PA.

———. 1827. "Valuable Property for Rent." *Oracle of Dauphin*, November 27.

———. 1842. "Last Will and Testament." New Bloomfield Court House. Filed May 16, 1855. microfilm C-85. Lenig Library, Perry Historians, Newport, PA.

Commonwealth of Pennsylvania. *An Act to Establish a Ferry Over the River Susquehanna, at or Near the Mounth of Juniata, and to Vest the Right thereof in Matthias Flam and David Watts, Their Heirs Assigns.* 1799. The Statutes at Large of Pennsylvania from 1682 to 1801. vol. XVI. Harrisburg: State of Pennsylvania.

———. n.d. *Historic Context for Transportation Networks in Pennsylvania.* Pennsylvania Department of Transportation. https://www.dot7.state.pa.us/CRGIS_Attachments/Survey/Transportation_Networks_Historic_Context.pdf (accessed October 15, 2017).

———. 1800. "Septennial Census Records for Rye Township, Cumberland County, PA." Harrisburg, Pennsylvania : Pennsylvnaia Historical and Museum Commission.

———. 1820. *Susquehanna and Part of Juniata from Genl. Watts Place on the Juniata to Wrights Ferry.* May 11. map #1892, A15, cabinet 7, drawer D1. Pennsylvania State Archives. Harrisburg, PA.

Commonwealth of Pennsylvania. Board of Canal Commissioners. Map Book 1810–1881. RG-17. Copied Surveys. Series 452. PHMC. http://www.phmc.state.pa.us (accessed February 7, 2018).

———. n.d. Duncan's Island, Section of Canal. PHMC. http://www. phmc.state.pa.us (accessed February 7, 2018).

Commonwealth of Pennsylvania. Deparment of Military Affairs. "Record of Burial Place of Veteran, Perry County." 22 March 1937. Harrisburg, PA.

Commonwealth of Pennsylvania. Land Office. 1768. Surveys. 1681–1912 [series #17.114]. RG-17, Records of the Land Office. PHMC. Harrisburg, PA. http://www.phmc.state. pa.us (accessed June 30, 2015).

———. 1769. Patent Index. AA-No. 10. PHMC. Harrisburg, PA. http://www.phmc .state.pa.us (accessed June 30, 2015).

———. 1813. Survey Map for Robert Clark. Book B-2-103. Pennsylvania Historical and Musuem Commission. April 5. http://www.phmc.state.pa.us (accessed July 14, 2015).

———. 1815. Survey Map for Robert Clark. Book C-28-281. Pennsylvania Historical and Museum Commission. July 20. http://www.phmc.state.pa.us (accessed July 14, 2015).

———. 1819. Survey Map for Robert Clark. Book B-2-104. Pennsylvania Historical and Museum Commission. October 5. http://www.phmc.state.pa.us (accessed July 14, 2015).

———. 1819. Survey Map for Robert Clark. Book A-10-223. Pennsylvania Historical and Museum Commission. October 10. http://www.phmc.state.pa.us (accessed July 14, 2015)

———. n.d. Warrantee Township Maps - Penn Township. Pennsylvania Historic and Musuem Commission. http://www.phmc.state.pa.us (accessed June 30, 2015).

Commonwealth of Pennsylvania. Pennsylvania Historical and Museum Commision. 2015. "Georgian-style 1700–1800." August 25. http://www.phmc.statepa.us/portal/communities/architecture/styles/georgian.html (accessed November 17, 2017).

Commonwealth of Pennsylvania. Supreme Court. Middle District. 1876. case no. 57. John Rice and Christina his wife in their right, Applicants vs. Zachariah Rice. New Bloomfield: *Perry Freeman*.

Cotton, J. Randall. "Log Houses in America." *Old-House Journal*. January/February, 1990. 37–44.

Crews, Ed. 2007. *Drinking in Colonial America*. https://www.history.org/foundation/journal/holiday07/drink.cfm (accessed September 13, 2017).

Cumberland County Clerk of Courts. Tavern License Petitions. Clark's Tavern. 1801. August. Robert Clark. Cumberland County Archives, Carlisle, PA. I.D. #1801.062. www.ccpa.net (accessed Jan 15, 2018).

———. 1802. Robert Clark. August. #1802.063. www.ccpa.net (accessed Jan 15, 2018).

———. 1810. Robert Clark. April. #1810.088. www.ccpa.net (accessed Jan 15, 2018).

———. 1812. Robert Clark. April. #1812.080. www.ccpa.net (accessed Jan 15, 2018).

———. 1813. Robert Clark. April. #1813.078. www.ccpa.net (accessed Jan 15, 2018).

———. 1814. Joseph Robison. August. #1814.081. www.ccpa.net (accessed Jan 15, 2018).

———. 1815. Joseph Robison. April. #1815.096. www.ccpa.net (accessed Jan 15, 2018).

———. 1816. Robert Patton. Aug. #1816.100. www.ccpa.net (accessed Jan 15, 2018).

———. 1819. Henry Leman, Aug. #1819.124. www.ccpa.net (accessed Jan 15, 2018).

———. 1820. Henry Leyman, Aug. #1820.137. www.ccpa.net (accessed Jan 15, 2018).

Cumberland County Clerk of Courts. Tavern License Recommendations. Clark's Tavern. 1790. Daniel Clark. RG/024/2T. Boxes 1 and 2. Manuscript. 1790–1808. Pennsylvania State Archives, Harrisurg, PA.

———. 1794. Daniel Clark. RG/024/2T. Boxes 1 and 2. Manuscript. 1790–1808. Pennsylvania State Archives, Harrisurg, PA.

———. 1795. Daniel Clark. RG/024/2T. Boxes 1 and 2. Manuscript. 1790–1808. Pennsylvania State Archives, Harrisurg, PA.

———. 1797. Daniel Clark. RG/024/2T. Boxes 1 and 2. Manuscript. 1790–1808. Pennsylvania State Archives, Harrisurg, PA.

———. 1798. Daniel Clark. RG/024/2T. Boxes 1 and 2. Manuscript. 1790–1808. Pennsylvania State Archives, Harrisurg, PA.

———. 1799. Robert Clark. RG/024/2T. Boxes 1 and 2. Manuscript. 1790–1808. Pennsylvania State Archives, Harrisurg, PA.

———. 1800. Robert Clark. RG/024/2T. Boxes 1 and 2. Manuscript. 1790–1808. Pennsylvania State Archives, Harrisurg, PA.

———. 1801. Robert Clark. RG/024/2T. Boxes 1 and 2. Manuscript. 1790–1808. Pennsylvania State Archives, Harrisurg, PA.

———. 1802. Robert Clark. RG/024/2T. Boxes 1 and 2. Manuscript. 1790–1808. Pennsylvania State Archives, Harrisurg, PA.

Cumberland County Clerk of Courts. Road Dockets. Order to view a road from Hackets to Sandersons. August 8, 1788. Folder 2-120. Cumberland County Archives, Carlisle, PA.

———. 1797. Road Petition for Daniel Clark. Docket #7, pp. 120, 130 & 142. Cumberland County Archives, Carlisle, PA.

———. 1811. Quarter Sessions Docket #11, p. 278. April. Cumberland County Archives, Carlisle, PA.

Cumberland County Orphans' Court. Letters of Administration. Appointment of Robert Clark as Administrator of Daniel Clark's Estate. 1800 December 4. (Folder C-3). Cumberland County Archives, Carlisle, PA.

———. 1800. Inventory of the Estate of John Clark. May 7. microfilm roll C-039. Cumberland County Historical Society, Carlisle, PA.

———. 1801. Daniel Clark.'s Estate Inventory. March 5. microfilm roll C-098. Cumberland County Historical Society, Carlisle, PA.

———. 1802. Petition to Award and Inquest to Partition John Clark's 215 Acres of Land Among John's Seven Children. Pennsylvania Probate Records 1683–1794. vol. 3. pp. 358–359.

———. 1802. John Clark's Estate Settlement. October 10. Pennsylvania Probate Records 1683–1794. vol. 3. pp. 367–368.

———. 1802. Value of Clark's Tavern and Property. October 10. Pennsylvania Probate Records 1683–1794. vol. 3. pp. 367–368.

———. 1802 Robert Clark Appointed Guardian of Jane, Nancy and EPeter Clark. October 10. Pennsylvania Probate Records 1683–1794. vol. 3 pg. 366.

Cumberland County Prothonotary. 1798. Naturalization Appearance Docket, Case #156. August.

Cumberland County Archives, Carlisle, PA.

Cumberland County Recorder of Deeds. Samuel Goudy and Wife to John Clark. 1787. deed book H. vol. 1. microfilm roll 2-3. pg. 384. Cumberland County Historical Society. Carlisle, PA. January 23.

Cumberland County Commisioners. Tax Rate Books. 1786. Rye Township. microfilm roll 150. Cumberland County Historical Society, Carlisle, PA.

———. 1786, 1787, 1788, 1789. Tax Rates Books. microfilm roll 150. Cumberland County Historical Society, Carlisle, PA.

———. 1793, 1801. Tax Rates Books. microfilm roll 151. Cumberland County Historical Society, Carlisle, PA.

———. 1814. Tax Rates Books. microfilm roll 152. Cumberland County Historical Society, Carlisle, PA.

———. 1817. Tax Rates Books. microfilm roll 153. Cumberland County Historical Society, Carlisle, PA.

Cumberland County Commissioners. Tavern Records and Licenses. 1750–1850. CCPA Archives. https://ccweb.ccpa.net/archives/RecordGroups (accessed January 12, 2019).

Cutty. 2011. "Grain Volumes for Whiskey and Vodka". June 3. http:www.adiforums.com (accessed June 28, 2017).

Dauphin County Commissioners. 1797–1805. House of Entertainment & Taverm License Recommendations, 1790–1809. Harrisburg, PA.

Dauphin County Pennsylvania Recorder of Deeds. 1785. Marcus Huling to Thomas Huling. October 15. Family Search. http:www.familysearch.org (accessed February 16, 2017).

———. 1804. Mathias Flam to Robert Clark. November 5. microfilm roll #1510, Book N, vol. 1, page 566, Pennsylvania State Archives. Harrisburg. PA.

———. 1837. Robert Clark and Wife, Maragaretta to Jacob Haldman. July and August. Book I, vol. 2, pp. 134–139. Family Search. http:www.familysearch.org (accessed February 4, 2019).

Dauphin County Board of Commissioners. Upper Paxton Township. Tax Rate Books. 1798. microfilm roll 4141. Family Search. http:www.familysearch.org (accessed September 29, 2017).

———. 1824 Halifax Township. Tax Rate Books. 1824. microfilm roll 4116. Family Search. http:www. family   search.org (accessed June 29, 2017)

———. 1827–1828. Halifax Township. Tax Rate Books. microfilm roll 4116. Family Search. http:www.family search.org (accessed June 29, 2017)

———. 1831–1837. Halifax Township. Tax Rate Books. microfilm roll 4116. Family Search.http:www.family search.org. (accessed June 29, 2017)

Distilled Spirits Council. 2017. *History of Spirits in America*. Distilled Spirits Council of the United States. www.discus.or/heritage/spirits/#2 (accessed June 28, 2017).

Douglas, Francis. 1782. *A General Description of the East Coast of Scotland*. Paisley: Alexander Weir.

Duncannon Record. 1974. "Owners of Old Tavern Seek Date." *Duncannon Record*: September 16.

Early American Life. "Setting an Early American Table." Chagrin Falls: Firelands Media Group, December 2004.

"Early Churches." 2003–2010. PaGenWeb. www.pagen.web/.org (accessed April 22, 2017).

Egle, William Henry, ed. *Notes and Queries :Historical, Biographical and Genealogical: Chiefly Relating to Interior Pennsylvania.* vol. 1. Harrisburg: Daily Telegraph, 1887.

Ellis, Franklin and Austin Hungerford. *History of that Part of the Susquehanna and Juniata Valleys, Embraced in the Counties of Mifflin, Juniata, Perry, Union and Snyder, in the Commonwealth of Pennsylvania.* vols. 1 and 2. Philadelphia: Everts, Peck & Richards, 1886.

Fairthorne, Mrs. Harry Boden IV. 1975. "Letter to Mrs. Janet Kliens." October 6. Boden File, Cumberland County Historical Society, Carlisle, PA.

Find A Grave, Inc. 1855. "Duncannon Presbyterian Cemetery." April 15. Find A Grave. https: www.findagrave.com (accessed March 18, 2017).

First National Bank of Newport. "Duncannon Perry County Pennsylvania...a History." Newport: First National Bank of Newport, 1987.

Flam, Mathias. 1800. "To the Public ." vol. VIII. no. XXXVII. Harrisburg: *Oracle of Dauphin,* July 12. 1.

Fletcher, S.W. "The Substence Farming Period in Pennsylvania Agriculture, 1640–1840." 1945. Journals.psu.edu. https://journals.psu.edu/phj/article/viewFile/21700/21469 (accessed March 3, 2017).

Frazer, Mrs. 1791. *The Practice of Cookery, Pastry, Pickling, Rreserving, &....* Edinburgh: Peter Hill .

Freeman. "Died at Clark's Ferry." April 26, 1855.

Garvin, James. *A Building History of Northern New England.* Hanover: University Press of New England, 2001.

Goudy, Samuel. "To Be Sold." *Carlisle Gazette.* vol. 1. no. 21. Carlisle, PA: Carlisle Gazette, December 27, 1785.

Graham, Henky Grey. *The Social Life of Scotland in the Eighteenth Century.* London: Adam and Charles Black, 1901.

Hain, Harry Harrison. *History of Perry County: Including Desriptions of Indians and Pioneer Life from the Time of Earliest Settlement, Sketches of its Noted Men and Women and Many Professional Men.* Perry County. PA: Hain-Moore Company, 1922.

Harrisburg Chronicle. June 24, 1833.

———. 2017. Harrisburg: History. June 12. www.city-data.com/us-cities/The-North east/Harrisburg-History.html (accessed 2017).

Hart, Victor, and Jason Wilson. "Clark's Ferry and Tavern; Gateway to the Juniata Valley." 2016. In *Pennsylvania History: A Journal of Mid-Atlantic Studies.* Ed.by Linda A. Ries (The Pennsylvania Historical Association and the Pennsylvania State University Press) 83 (2): 135–158.

Historic House Blog. "Historic Style Spotlight: The Craftsman Bungalow." August 2. 2012. www.historichouseblog.com/2012/08/02/historic-style-spotlight-the-crafts man-bungalow (accessed April 22, 2018).

Howell, Reading. "A Map of the State of Pennsylvania." 1792. Maps of Pennsylvania. http:// maps of pa.com/antiquemap29a.html (accessed August 8, 2017)

Huling, Marcus. 1762. Heratage Quest. http://countyof napa.org/library-databases (accessed April 3, 2017).

Jefferies, Joseph and John Wright. "To Our Friends." *Pennsylvania Chronicle*. Philadelphia: *Pennsylvania Chronicle*, December 7, 1787. In George Reeser Prowell. "River Ferries over the Susquehanna in 1787—Wright's and Anderson's." Lancaster: Lancaster Historical Society, 1923.

Jackson, Donald C. 2014. *Roads Most Traveled; Turnpikes in Southeastern Pennsylvania in the Early Republic*. ed by Judith McGaw. Chappel Hill: UNC Press Books, 197–239.

Johnstone, Lindsey. *Ten of the best Scottish food and drink proverbs*. September 18, 2015. Scotsman Food & Drink. foodanddrink.scotsman.com/drink/ten-of-the-best -scottish-food-and-drink-proverbs (accessed July 2, 2017).

Jones, U. J. *History of the Early Settlement of the Juniata Valley*. Harrisburg: Harrisburg Publishing Company, 1889.

Jordan, John W. *A History of the Juniata Valley and Its People*. vol. 2. New York: Lewis Historical Publishing, 1913.

Kelker, Luther Reily. *History of Dauphin County Pennsylvania*. vol. 1. New York: Lewis Publishing Company, 1907.

Kelley, Joseph J. *Life and Times in Colonial Philadelphia*. Harrisburg, Pennsylvania: Stackpole, 1973.

Kelly, James. *A Complete Collection of Scottish Provers Explained and Made Intelligible to the English Reader*. London: Rodwell & Martin, 1818.

Klines Gazette. "Died on Wednesday Last." September 24, 1800.

———. "Married Friday last at Clark's Ferry." June 20, 1804.

———. "Married last evening at Robert Clark's." November 29, 1811.

Leyburn, James G. *The Scotch-Irish: A Social History*. Chapel Hill: Univ. of North Carolina Press, 1989.

Long, Theodore K. *Forty Letters To Carson Long*. New Bloomfield: Carson Long Institute, 1931.

Masters, Frank M. "Notes & Data Relative to the Building of the Bridge Across the Susquehanna River at Clark's Ferry." October 3, 1925. Copy in Clark's Ferry Folder. Historical Society of Perry County. Newport, PA.

National Library of Scotland. 2017. Recipies from Scotland; 1680's to 1940's. digital.nis.uk/recipes/themes/index.html (accessed July 4, 2017).

Ohio History Central. "Northwest Territory." 2015. Ohio History Central. http://www.ohio historycentral.org/w/Northwest_Territory?rec=772 (accessed August 15, 1016).

Old Timer. "The Letter Box," c. 1870. Perry Historians, Newport , Pennsylvania.

Oracle of Dauphin. "To the Public." July 12, 1800.

———. "Died on Wednesday last." September 22, 1800.

———. "Mortuary Notice of Mr. John Clark." vol. X. no. 44. August 30, 1802.

Pencak, William."The Promise of Rvolutions:1750–1800." In *Pennsylvania: A History of the Commonwealth*, Ed. Randall M.: Pencak, Miller, 105–152. University Park: Pennsylvania University Press.

Pennsylvania U.S.Geological Survey. *Perry County, Penn (Wheatfield and Rye) Township*. US Gen Web Pennsylvania Archives. September 8, 2009. usgwarchieves.net/maps /pa/county/perry/usgs (accessed March 8, 2017).

Perry County. October, 2013. Perry County, Pennsylvania. www.perryco.org /Documents/05-FLOODING.pdf (accessed June 12, 2017).

Perry County Democrat. "Robert Clarks Death." New Bloomfield: Perry County Democrat, April 26, 1855.

———. "Sheriff Sale." March 3, 1880.

Perry County Board of Commissioners, Tax Rate Books, 1840, 1841, 1842, 1843, 1849, 1850, 1853, Penn Township, Lenig Library, Perry Historians, New Bloomfield, PA.

———. 1829–1830, Wheatfield Township, FamilySearch, https://www. familysearch .org/search/catalog (accessed March 27, 2019)

Perry County Recorder of Deeds. 1869. Margaretta and Zachariah Rice to William King, Joseph Swartz & John Shively. Book 2-B. pp. 318–319. New Bloomfield, PA. April 12.

———. 1875. William King, Joseph Swartz amd John Shively to David and Enos Smith. book J. vol. II. p 289. New Bloomfield, PA.

———. 1880. Recorder of Deeds. *Sheriff Sale*. "J.A. Gray to Enos Smith et. al." 1880. microfilm roll 192. Perry Historian Library. New Bloomfield, PA.

———. 2012. Landex2012205944. New Bloomfield, PA. July 30.

———. 2015. Agreement for Clark's Ferry Tavern Property. Borough of Duncannon to the Perry County Historical Society. September 23.

Perry Forester. 1822. "Robert Clark a Member of the Domocratic Republican Committee." July 25.

———. 1820. "Robert Clark, Rye Townships Justice of the Peace." Landisburg: Perry Forester , December 16.

Rice, Kim S. *Early American Taverns: For the Entertainment of Friends and Strangers*. Chicago: Regnery Gateway, 1983.

Rowlett, Russ. 2001. *A Dictonary of Units of Measurement*. University of North Carolina at Chapel Hill. www.unc.edu/rowlett/units/scales/bushels.html (accessed June 28, 2017).

Sanborn Map Company. 1894. *Sanborn Fire Insurance Map of Duncannon, Perry County, Pennsylvania*. August Library of Congress. https://www.loc.gov/resource /g3824dm.g3824dm_g076301894/?st=gallery (accessed November 23, 2017).

Scotch Malt Whisky Forum. 2017. The History of Scotch Whisky. www.scotchmalt whisky.co.uk (accessed April 30, 2017).

Scotch Whiskey Association. 2012. History of Scotch Whisky. May 31. http://www .scotch-whisky.org. uk/understanding-scotch/history-of-whisky/(accessed April 30, 2017).

Scull, William. *A Map of Pennsylvania Exhibiting Not Only the improved parts of that Province, but Also its extensive Frontiers.* London : Robet Sayer & J. Bennett, 1775.

Shank, William H. *The Amazing Pennsylvania Canals.* York: American Canal and Transportation Center, 1981

Shultz, Suzanne M. "Epidemics in Colonial Americafrom 1699–1799 and the Risk of Dyng." *Archiving Early America.* 2007–2017. http://www.varsitytutors.com /earlyamerica/early-america.../early-american-epidemics (accessed March 8, 2017).

Shumway, George, et al. *Conestoga Wagon 1750–1850: Freight Carrier for 100 Years of Americas Westward Expansion.* York: Early American Indistries Association, 1964.

Smith, Thomas, Samuel Harrison, and John Melish. 1816. *Map of Dauphin & Lebanaon counties: contructed by virtue of and Act of the Legislature of Pennsylvania.* Pennsylvania Historical and Museum Commission. www.phmc.state.pa.us/bah /dam/rg/di/r17/-WhitesidesMaps/m011Map0082DauphinLebanon.pdf (accessed October 16, 2016).

Sneed, David. "Wheels That Won the West." East to West. 2015–2016. http//www .wheelsthat wonthewest.com (accessed September 18, 2016).

"Social History of Scotland." n.d. *Category Archives: 17th and 18th Centuries.* www.nick loggie.com/category/17th-and-18th-centuries/ (accessed December 17, 2017).

Somerville, Thomas. *My Own Life and Times, 1741–1830.* Edinburgh:Edmonston & Douglas, 1861.

Staff, History.com. *Conestoga Wagon.* A+E Networks. 2010. http://www.history.com /topics/conestoga-wagon (accessed December 22, 2016).

Stewart, Ms. Terry. "The Highland Clearances." 2017. Historic UK. http://www .historic-uk.com/HistoryUK/History of Scotland/ (accessed July 2, 2017).

Struzinski, Steven. 2002. "The Tavern in Colonial America." *The Gettysburg Historical Journal* (Gettysburg College) 1 (7).

Toland, Bill. 2007. "Rye is Popular Again." Post Gazette. May 23. http://www.post -gazetter.com/ libations/2007/05/23/Rye (accessed April 30 , 2017).

U.S. Direct Tax of 1798 for Cumberland County Rye Township. National Archives and Records Administration. microfilm roll 17. Cumberland County Historical Society. Carlisle, PA.

U.S. Secretary of State. 1800 Decennial Census. Cumberland County, Rye Township, PA. U.S. National Archives and Records Adminsitration. FamilySearch. https: //www.familysearch.org (accessed November 29, 2017).

———. 1810 Decennial Census. Cumberland County, Rye Township, PA. U.S. National Archives and Records Adminsitration. FamilySearch. https: //www.family search.org (accessed November 29, 2017).

———. 1840. Decennial Census. Perry County, Saville Township, PA. U.S. National Archives and Records Adminsitration. FamilySearch. https: //www.familysearch .org (accessed November 29, 2017).

U.S. Department of the Interior. 1850 Decennial Census. Perry County, Saville Township. series M432, microfilm roll 805. Pennsylvania State Archives. Harrisburg, PA.

Visser, Thomas. 1997. "Nails: Cluest to a Building's History ." *University of Vermont Historic Preservation Program, Historic Preservation Research*. University of Vermont. http://www.uvm.edu/-histpres/203/nails.html (accessed October 30, 2017).

Watson, Alan D. 2001. "Transportation." *The Colonial Records Project*. May 1. Colonial Williamsburg. www.ncpublications.com/colonial/Nchr/Subjects/watson20.htm (accessed December 2, 2016).

Way, George. *Scottish Clan & Family Encyclopedia*. Glasgow: HarperCollins, 1994.

Wilkinson, Norman, and George Beyer. 1997. *The Conestoga Wagon*. Leaflet No. 5, Commonwealth of Pennsylvania. Harrisburg: Pennsylvania Historical and Museum Commission.

Winthrop, Grace. 1987. "Early Inns and Taverns." *History Quartily Digital Archives*, Tredyffrin Easttown Historical Society. 25 (3): 79–91. http://www.tehistory.org (accessed February 2, 2017).

Wright, Silas B. *History of Perry County, Pennsylvania: From the Earliest Settlement to the Present Time*. Harvard: Wylie and Griest, 1873.

Wright's to Juniata Map. May 11, 1820. Map #1892, A15, Cabinet 7, Drawer D1, Pennsylvania State Archives. Harrisburg, PA.

INDEX

ABOUT THE AUTHOR

Victor Hart is a retired secondary history teacher with a combined thirty-one years of teaching experience in Washington, DC, Texas, Maryland, and Pennsylvania. For twelve years, he was the Archaeological Director for the Historical Society of Perry County. He is a 1967 graduate of George Washington University with a BA in history, a 1979 graduate of the University of the Americas with an MA in anthropology. He also completed numerous post-graduate courses in education, archaeology, and museum studies. He is the coauthor of *Clark's Ferry and Tavern: Gateway to the Juniata Valley* and *Digging for the Clarks: A Four Year Community Archaeological Excavation at Clark's Ferry Tavern (2012–2015)*.

Made in the USA
Middletown, DE
21 December 2020